Can A Gluten-Free Diet Help? How?

Can A
GLUTEN-FREE
DIET HELP?
How?

Lloyd Rosenvold, M.D.

Keats Publishing, Inc. New Canaan, Connecticut

Can a Gluten-Free Diet Help? How? is not intended as medical advice. Its intent is solely informational and educational. Please consult a health professional should the need for one be indicated.

Library of Congress Cataloging-in-Publication Data

Rosenvold, Lloyd.
   Can a gluten-free diet help? How? / Lloyd Rosenvold.
   p.   cm.
   ISBN 0-87983-538-9 : $9.95
   1. Celiac disease—Diet therapy. 2. Gluten-free diet. I. Title.
RC862.C44R67   1992
615.8'54—dc20
                                          90-23369
                                          CIP

Printed in the United States of America

Published by Keats Publishing, Inc.
27 Pine Street (Box 876)
New Canaan, Connecticut 06840-0876

CONTENTS

INTRODUCTION

THE MISSING DIAGNOSIS

There are multiplied millions of Americans with obscure, often grave, and sometimes disabling symptoms. Many of these individuals do not receive a definitive diagnosis of their condition, and hence too often less than adequate treatment. Worse yet, at times, the wrong treatment.

This is not necessarily due to carelessness in diagnosis and "sloppy" medical practice. The fact is, there are certain medical conditions which can be extremely difficult to identify, thus leading to a delay in arriving at an accurate diagnosis.

Thousands of these individuals may appear to be in reasonably acceptable health, but they may be functioning far "below par" in strength and purpose. They become discouraged and depressed over the fact that others do not seem to understand their weakness and distress. Blood tests and X-ray studies may reveal no clearly identifiable disease. Poking and prodding by the physician may uncover nothing really diagnostic.

Too often these patients are labelled psychoneurotics or hypochondriacs and they may be referred to psychologists or psychiatrists for mental evaluation. Many end up being placed on various tranquilizer-type drugs and may be subjected to multiple and extended counselling sessions at a huge expense. The mood swings that are so common in some of these frustrating conditions are not necessarily of the common mental or emotional origin. Instead they may be based on *real* physical distress, and no amount of counselling will cure them.

WRONGFUL TREATMENTS

Some of these unfortunate patients have been subjected to unnecessary surgical procedures which have actually for a time seemed to benefit and encourage these patients. How can this be? We will tell you how, based upon valid physiological explanations. We don't recommend unnecessary operations and treatments, but if such have been instituted we should learn lessons from them and find diagnostic and therapeutic wisdom from them.

Family members often misunderstand the sufferers and cannot figure out why the husband or wife is not able to carry his or her responsibilities. Great weakness may persist, while vague complaints or symptoms abound. Some of the symptoms which we will relate may have multiple causes. However, we will focus principally on *four* well-known conditions that are frequently overlooked or misdiagnosed and are indeed at times very difficult for anyone to diagnose in the earlier stages.

FOUR DISEASES: SO MUCH IN COMMON

These four diseases are distinct and are considered to be unrelated, yet at the same time they have *so much in common*, and in some patients are so interrelated that two or more of these conditions may coexist in the same patient. No wonder that sometimes even very fine medical specialists find it difficult to make a definitive diagnosis.

In all four conditions the immune system of the body is involved and compromised, and in all four the central nervous system is also involved, albeit not in an identical manner in each instance. Yet, they all have the common feature of immune system involvement.

As I shall name these four, I realize that some of my medical fellow practitioners may think that I have lost my mind in so closely associating the four. But hold on! Hear me out! There is indeed much overlapping in the four and we all need to recognize this as we sort out the symptoms and findings in arriving at a differential and then final diagnosis.

The four diseases are: gluten intolerance (also known as celiac sprue, and indeed hereafter we will abbreviate celiac sprue as CS and the abbreviation will also stand for *gluten intolerance*); multiple sclerosis (MS); gastro-intestinal yeast infection (YI); and finally, myasthenia gravis (MG).

Right now I can hear some readers express their doubt that there is any connection or commonality between the four, but hold on, wait and see! You may be astounded. We will carefully document some of their interrelationships with suitable references and case reports.

Why This Book?

Clearly, while this book deals primarily with celiac sprue (gluten intolerance) it is not intended to be a definitive text on the topic. The finest available text on celiac sprue of which I am aware is the book *On the Celiac Condition,* by Leon Rottmann, Ph.D. It is available from the Celiac Sprue Association, United States of America. See the Appendix for more information.

This book deals briefly with signs and symptoms of CS, just enough to aid readers who are not versed on the disease, by giving them a brief overview so that they can follow the chapters with some basic comprehension. But Dr. Rottmann's manual is by far a better basic textbook.

The principal purpose of my volume is to call attention to a definite connection or relationship between celiac sprue and other diseases such as multiple sclerosis and intestinal yeast infection, as well as certain other medical problems. To my knowledge, these relationships have not been extensively explored in medical literature.

I report herein cases of multiple sclerosis patients who at the same time suffer from celiac sprue; or if some would prefer that we turn the equation around, cases of CS that also have MS. Either way we state it the relationship needs to be explored and studied.

Similarly, I am convinced that the relationship between intestinal yeast infection and CS also needs to be further explored and clarified, even though some writers seem to minimize the relationship, calling it "infrequent." My evaluation is that it is a large relationship.

I hope this current report will stimulate research on the part of others to determine whether the illustrative cases we have reported are simply rare anomalies, or if such relationships are more common than we have ever dreamed. I am inclined to believe the latter. The paragraph which follows constitutes a brief encouragement to lay readers and patients to be alert to their own needs and to become knowledgeable about CS and related topics.

YOUR MEDICAL DESTINY

Customarily, physicians are thought to be in charge of the medical and health destiny of their patients. But should this really be so? *You* as the patient are in charge of your own body. The physician and his staff, your family and friends serve as helpers, consultants. Never forget that you must take an active interest in your bodily welfare. This is especially true in the instance of the immune system diseases which we will be discussing in this volume. Self-help is so exceedingly vital to you. Do not forfeit your responsibility to oversee your own medical welfare. Become informed so that you can make decisions with propriety. It is our hope that this book will help you to appreciate the importance of your own self-help.

A MEDICAL CURIOSITY?

It was more than a half century ago that my pediatrics professor in the medical college introduced us rather briefly to a curious intestinal affliction of small children, called celiac disease, wherein the child developed poorly owing to his severe digestive disturbances.

It was not a seemingly common condition at that time and at the moment he had no clinical cases on hand for purposes of demonstration. Back in that era the condition seemed to be somewhat of a medical curiosity. Yes, there was knowledge concerning the condition, but it seemed to be of interest only to a few physicians in various countries, being more common in England.

Since in due time I entered into a medical specialty field other than one involving intestinal diseases, it was not until a few decades later that I would come face to face with the condition in family members and realize in retrospect that celiac disease has been with the human race for centuries, but is much misunderstood and too often goes unrecognized. In the intervening decades most medical journals seemed totally silent on the topic. Today journals are not so silent, fortunately.

Indeed, much of the progress in dissemination of facts and general recognition of the widespread incidence of celiac disease or celiac sprue came about as a result of diligent and persistent research on the part of sufferers with CS, sparked prominently in the U.S.A. by energetic groups of CS victims in the midwestern states who banded themselves together to share experiences and knowledge, and to enlist the help of able intestinal specialists in their cause.

From their early efforts has now developed the Celiac Sprue Association/U.S.A. with headquarters in Omaha, Nebraska. Their apt slogan is "Celiacs helping celiacs," as they share information, experiences and observations with each other through medical conventions and various publications. Similar associations of celiacs are found in various parts of North America. (Hereinafter we will occasionally refer to patients who have celiac sprue as "celiacs"—a synonym. Celiac sprue and celiac disease are also synonyms.)

1

WHAT IS CELIAC SPRUE?

Celiac Sprue (CS) is a relatively uncommon, familial, inborn error of the digestive metabolism that is obviously genetically mediated. It manifests itself principally in an inability of the small bowel (mostly in the jejunum portion) to digest and absorb gluten-containing foods such as wheat, rye, barley and oats. The proper digestive enzymes for these glutens appear to be completely lacking, or else in short supply, in the bowels.

Many other foods also contain a gluten protein—corn, for example. But it is the *alpha-gliadin* portion of the above four gluten grains that is the offending factor. When we speak of "portion" (singular) we are, in the case of wheat, actually speaking of as many as 40 different gliadins. It would appear that the damage potential of these 40 varieties varies in the limited tests conducted thus far. Testing procedures are very complicated and laborious. Actually, in the tests cited, only four of the 40 components were critically tested. Grains such as corn *do not* contain the alpha-gliadin. Some varieties of millet and buckwheat also appear to contain alpha-gliadin.

Not only are the *alpha*-gliadin gluten foods themselves improperly absorbed, but secondarily, incidental to the deranged intraintestinal function, almost *all* nutrients (including miner-

1

als) tend to absorb poorly from the bowels (particularly the jejunum portion). This is especially true of fats. Accordingly, varying degrees of malnutrition afflict CS patients. What's more, toxic or incompletely digested food components are absorbed into the bloodstream to adversely affect distant organs and functions.

To re-emphasize, it's the *alpha-gliadin portion of the gluten protein* peculiar to the aforementioned four grains that is the offending factor in these otherwise nutritionally superior grains. Glutens of other plant foods that do not contain the alpha-gliadin fraction are *not* offenders.

Since CS is a genetically transmitted affliction, we can expect digestive disturbances to surface quite soon after gluten foods are added to a baby's diet. In most instances the condition tends to be misdiagnosed as various diagnostic labels are hung on the ailing infant. As the child develops during childhood and the teens, the intestinal disturbances may *seem* to disappear, but later in middle adult life they reappear and may eventually and belatedly be recognized as CS. Virtually no two patients have the same case history.

SOME ANATOMY

The small intestines are lined by mucous membranes consisting of millions of microscopic hair-like processes with their intervening spaces, giving the lining a velvet-like appearance. The convoluted projections, called *villi*, increase the surface area of the intestinal lining by enormous proportions by their convolutions, thus increasing the surface contact with the food ingested.

In CS these villi are damaged and often destroyed. Accordingly, the surface area of the lining may be reduced by as much as 75 percent, and one authority states that in some cases 99.5 percent of all the former functional jejunal surface area may have been lost. This means that the ability to digest and absorb food in those areas is lost to an equal extent.

There are various theories as to *how* gluten damages the intestinal lining. The most currently accepted theory is that the alpha-gliadin fraction of the gluten combines with the abnormal genes in the cells of the intestinal mucous membrane forming toxic substances that destroy the lining membranes and the villi. Malabsorption and malnutrition follow. Additionally, toxic substances can be absorbed into the general blood circulation and be transported to distant tissues to wreak further havoc.

When a celiac patient eats the offending gluten, immune system lymphocytes from the mucous lining (and from the bloodstream) sally forth to try to destroy the offending gluten. That is by nature their protective work. But, through what we might call a misguided immune response, they end up destroying the small intestine (jejunum) lining instead. This is an auto-immune response—a body's reaction *against* its *own* tissues. Some kind of faulty genetic stimulus initiates the perverted response.

If the patient is young enough and the offending foods are excluded early enough, the intestinal lining may, to a great degree, regenerate itself. But the exclusion of the alpha-gliadin must be vigorous, thorough and sustained. The tendency of the tissues to react to the substance can *never* be cured. That's a part of the genetic make-up of the individual.

ON AGAIN, OFF AGAIN

If a patient were to faithfully exclude gluten for a long enough time the intestinal lining would no doubt to a great extent regenerate the villi and he would probably experience great improvement and be so jubilant that he might conclude that he was "cured." Or the next practitioner whom he consults might even tell him that he does not have CS, for he no longer evidences the typical symptoms. If the patient then returns to a use of the offending gluten foods he may at first notice no distress and then he feels totally confident that he no longer has CS as formerly believed.

But the reintroduced gluten is doing its harmful work and suddenly his CS symptoms return, perhaps more severe than ever. The villi are once again being destroyed. Then, if he once again adopts the gluten-free diet his intestinal lining may recover once more. But if this process of "on again, off again" is repeated too many times, scar tissue will develop and the tissues will finally refuse to heal and regenerate. The patient may end up with a very distressing, permanent condition which need not have developed had he been faithfully following a gluten-free diet program.

We cannot stress too strongly: The basic genetic defect that allows the intestinal condition to develop is never cured. Therefore, it's imperative that the patient enter upon the GF diet as soon as a reliable diagnosis has been made, and then *stay on the diet principles for life!*

Allergies

A few words about food allergy. Gluten intolerance is not a true "allergy" in the classical sense of the term, even though there seems to be an antigen-antibody kind of reaction taking place in the bowel lining. But, after CS becomes well-established, the impaired bowels may give evidence of allergy or hypersensitivity to an ever-increasing number of other foods, such as: tomato, soybean products and milk products. These are probably secondary to the long-standing failure of the digestive processes. Additionally, the patient may of course become allergic to the other various proteins found in the grains.

Two Suspected Foods

For years there has been a vigorous discussion among celiac circles about whether buckwheat and millet should be considered forbidden foods for celiacs and whether or not they contain the alpha-gliadin factor in their gluten. Millet is, of course, a grain of the grass family. Some have claimed that some varieties are tolerated and others not. It's probably the safest for CS patients to *not* use millet.

As for buckwheat, some authorities claim it contains the alpha-gliadin factor. Anyone who has watched buckwheat grow in a field will know that it is not a narrow-leafed plant like the grasses but has broad leaves. Rather then engaging in controversy over the buckwheat, it's probably safest for celiacs to exclude it also. In the remainder of this book we will basically refer to the four main offenders but keep in mind in the background the possibility, or probability, that these two additional "grains" *might* also be offenders.

A NEW NON-OFFENDER?

There is a "new" seed "grain" on the scene, namely the Quinoa plant which is native to South America but is now being grown in North America. It is from a plant of the Chenopodium family and it appears to be compatible with diets for celiacs. We have used it for a number of years without any demonstrable clinical adverse effects. As far as I know no definitive chemical tests have been done to determine the presence or absence of alpha-gliadin. The quinoa plant, I am told, is botanically related to the common garden weed, lamb's quarters. Thus it does not belong to the grass family as do the four principal offending grains.

Quinoa (pronounced keeń-wah) makes a delicious cooked breakfast gruel or mush and it can be ground into flour and used in baking. The firm that introduced the "grain" into the U.S. now makes elbow macaroni pasta which is also delicious. Quinoa has not as yet been laboratory tested for alpha-gliadin, but clinically it appears to be well-tolerated.

THE GENETIC CONNECTION

That celiac sprue is a genetic disease appears to be a given. One competent investigator has stated:

> Approximately 10 percent of first-degree relatives are found
> to have latent [celiac] sprue. In the general population only
> 6 percent are found to have the genetic markers. . . .
> —Rowell Setterman, M.D.; CSA/USA Bulletin 5:11, 1987

In other words, if there is a family member with CS the probability of another closely related member having the CS genetic markers is increased. One figure which I have heard quoted is that there is a 40 percent possibility of another member having the genetic trait if others in the family have the trait. The accuracy of this figure I cannot vouch for.

Two Astounding Families

We have records of two parallel families where two brothers from a very large family married two sisters, also from a large family. Thus two families were established which we shall refer to as "primary" families.

Apparently the genetic matches were a disaster! In one of these primary families three sisters have CS and at the same time all three have multiple sclerosis (MS) that has been proven. One brother (now deceased from other causes) also had proven MS. Some of his offspring have evidences of MS. A number of the offspring of these families have MS and some have evidences of CS.

In the other primary family there are at least two positively proven cases of MS. One sibling has CS and she has one offspring with clear evidences of CS. There are other descendants of both primary families who have symptoms suggestive of CS and/or MS, but we have not had access to their medical records.

Clearly, the two original gene pools, which were not blood related in any way, somehow must have had genes for both MS and CS in rich abundance. As far as family history is concerned one of the mothers in one primary family did have severe rheumatoid arthritis (another autoimmune disorder) and there is some evidence that perhaps she might have had CS as well. But this was never medically established. There is no other family history suggesting any distant relatives with known CS or MS.

An obvious question arises. If both CS and MS can be hereditarily traced in these two primary families, to say nothing of other suspected cases in more distant relatives for which there has not been opportunity to do accurate tracing and proving, could it be that in some way the genetic markers of CS and MS are related? We don't have a definitive answer to this question but we believe that common sense should dictate that perhaps patients with CS should be checked for possible MS and vice versa. We will give further details of some of these family members in other chapters.

Members of the two primary families can trace more than 100 first cousins in the total collateral families. One of the family members, herself having both MS and CS, has carried on an informal telephone and correspondence survey of most of the more than 100 first cousins and has reported to this writer an unusually large number who have medical and personal histories that contain presumptive evidence of possible CS, possible MS, or both. This is *in addition* to those formally diagnosed as either MS or CS.

But since these surveys were quite informal and have not been checked by medical findings, we can only report that the genetic pools from which the two primary families emerged seem to have had more than the usual percentage of possible genetic markers for CS and for MS.

As we've cited earlier, some authorities speak of ten percent of inheritance that can be traced in CS. Our only reply is that the two primary families show a percentage that must be many times that figure. One of the female cases in one of those families has two daughters. Both have proven MS. Neither has been critically examined for CS.

Is there a genetic connection between MS and CS? The experience of these two primary families would suggest that there must be some kind of connection.

2

ONE DISEASE, MANY SYMPTOMS

SYMPTOMS OF CS

There are multitudinous numbers of symptoms that are found to be clearly suggestive or even typical of CS, especially so if they are found in certain combinations. Understandably, each person will evidence symptoms somewhat different from another patient. We will name only a few of the main symptoms which should alert physicians and readers alike to the possibility of CS being present. Some of our case reports will further elucidate symptomatology.

In brief, the symptoms of celiac sprue include:

Nausea, vomiting (especially in infants and children)
Bloating and abdominal distention
Chronic diarrhea or, conversely,
Chronic constipation
Severe flatulence
Passing unformed stools or stools that are very bulky
Bleeding from the colon
Fatigue

Muscle weakness and wasting of the muscles
Depression and/or low self-esteem
Memory loss, inability to concentrate

These symptoms often begin in childhood (often starting after weaning), with the depression or discouragement emerging later as the condition continues unrecognized and untreated. Celiacs may have a few or many of the above symptoms.

The situation gets even more complicated as symptoms of nutritional deficiencies (brought on because the celiac's body is not absorbing nutrients from the food he eats) occur, giving rise to other conditions caused by malnutrition.

Abdominal Symptoms

The most classical symptoms are found in the gastro-intestinal tract. Severe flatulence and abdominal distention, to the extent that the clothing waistbands become too tight, are common complaints. The intestinal gas is so voluminous that the person may be unable to control it in public, and it's often so foul in odor that both patient and family can hardly endure the odor. We know of one case where a patient's gas was so foul that the family dog who liked to lie on his lap would leave the lap when the gas was expelled, and dogs are not usually averse to bad odors. One has to live with someone with this severe affliction in order to appreciate how utterly disabling and frustrating the flatulence condition can be for the whole family.

Severe diarrhea is very common, but in other cases the rule may be severe constipation. One 30-year-old man told us that he had never had a normal bowel movement as long as he could remember. Some pass only pellets rather than formed stools, while others may pass bulky stools. One young lady was known to clog flush toilets with her bulky stools.

A young mother with two children (herself a celiac victim) has related how her 3-year-old son had had only one—yes, one—formed fecal stool in his three years of life. She has suspected that he too has celiac disease and is investigating the possibility by testing him as well as his sister on gluten-free diets. She is proceeding in a logical manner to test the possibilities.

With all of the irritation from the diarrhea, the lower bowel becomes severely irritated, raw and inflamed. Bleeding from the colon is not uncommon and this tendency is further aggravated by the deficient absorption of the fat-soluble vitamin K which is involved in facilitating blood clotting.

Some authorities believe that colon cancer is more frequent in celiacs. Others say no. The jury is still out on this question.

Musculoskeletal

Some patients with CS have musculoskeletal symptoms of various types. In later essays we will introduce the possible connection between CS and arthritis, poly-myositis, and also bursitis. There seems to be a degree of commonality between these autoimmune diseases and celiac sprue, which also has autoimmune features.

Some of the latest research indicates that diarrhea is not always a constant to look for in making the diagnosis of celiac disease. (Neither for that matter is constipation. In some infants, slow growth and development or failure to thrive might be the tell-tale evidence that celiac disease should be considered.)

Once again we stress that we are not trying to exhaustively list all of the diagnostic factors to be considered in evaluating a suspected case of CS. Besides the medical history and symptoms of a CS suspect, there is a laboratory test that is available. The patient swallows an instrument which is passed through the stomach and several feet into the small intestines where a kind of "punch" or "suction" biopsy is taken of the intestinal lining. This specimen is then retrieved and subjected to laboratory analysis.

The test is only of value if done properly and a suitable specimen is obtained. Also, the patient must be actively consuming gluten at the time. The test is further limited by the fact that it is not readily available in every medical facility, and lastly, it is also limited in practicability because it is relatively expensive. Many CS suspects cannot afford the test.

A more recent test involves examining the duodenum by direct vision through fiber-optic scopes. Visible changes in the mucosal folds indicate a need for a biopsy. New blood tests for celiac sprue are in the works but not yet standardized.

Unfortunately, American physicians are not that aware of celiac disease. Some critics charge the doctors are so preoccupied with diagnosing pancreatitis, even when in some cases there is no pancreatitis to diagnose. It is difficult for a clinician to spot celiac disease, since it is one of the great "mimics" in the field of medicine. Diagnosis can be quite complicated.

THE DEFINITIVE TEST

In the end, the definitive or final test is the "eating test." This is conducted at home by the subject who must eliminate *all* traces of wheat, rye, barley and oats in any form, as well as derivatives of the four grains. This must be done very meticulously. Every tiny morsel of these foods must be excluded. Even such simple things as "malt" flavoring listed on packages of corn flakes disqualifies the food from use.

Tablets that might contain any of these food sources must also be excluded. Every possible source of alpha-gliadin gluten in any form or amount must be excluded. Whether the biopsy test is negative or positive, the only test that is definitive is the eating test. It may sound less scientific than the biopsy test, but it is the *real* test.

In some cases of CS dramatic results may be experienced in as little time as 36 hours. In other cases it may require weeks before relief can be obtained and one can conclude that indeed the subject does have celiac sprue.

The Milk Factor

Because the lactose in milk (milk sugar) and milk products causes some reactions in the bowel that mimic the gluten reactions, we advise test subjects to exclude milk from the test diet unless the specially treated Lactaid milk is available. Soy products are likewise in some cases associated with the CS problem, therefore soy foods should be excluded from the test diet. There is more on the connection between lactose intolerance and gluten intolerance later in this chapter.

Extreme Sensitivity

So that readers may appreciate how exceedingly sensitive the intestinal tissues are to gluten we cite the case of a celiac who was doing nicely on her gluten-free (GF) diet until, at church service, she ate one *very tiny* piece of wheat communion bread. She became ill and it took seven weeks for her bowels to recover. Another similar patient ate gluten bread while on vacation and it took her weeks to recover. Another at a picnic absentmindedly ate one bite of a wheat sandwich and became quite ill with a severe diarrhea. Another person became ill merely from some wheat bread crumbs that a family member had allowed to fall into the butter tub on the table. Will the body react to tiny amounts of gluten? It surely will, as these examples demonstrate.

CONDUCTING THE TEST

If possible, record all foods eaten for several days before commencing the test diet. Then record every morsel of food eaten during the days of the test (by name, not by weight). By keeping an accurate record of food intake and symptoms experienced (or not experienced) it will become easier to evaluate results.

If there is relief of symptoms, these findings point toward the diagnosis of celiac sprue. If there are no beneficial effects from the test diet we can conclude that the subject probably does *not* have CS. The test should then be discontinued. For more details on how to make your diet gluten-free, see the last chapter, Where to Begin.

It's astounding how few persons are willing to undertake so relatively simple a test as this home self-test. Most persons want nothing to do with diets—even test diets that take only a few days to conduct. A few years ago I conversed with and described this test to a wheelchair-ridden multiple sclerosis victim, suggesting that the test might be helpful—just as an exploratory measure. He was being treated with strong drugs and his outlook was not good. But he showed no interest whatever in the test.

Another person who had opportunity to take the test was not the least bit interested. Several years later she is now confined to her wheelchair for her MS and if she falls she must somehow crawl to the telephone and call for help to be lifted up.

It's so sad that persons will try almost any drug or any treatment, as long as it does not touch their taste buds or stomach. They want no re-education of their appetite. Not even a simple home test to find out if maybe a change in diet could help. That seems to be human nature. Some would seemingly rather die than risk finding out that maybe—just maybe—a diet change could be beneficial. Human nature is so strange. But this writer hopes that this volume will reach a few souls who are at least willing to search for a better way of life through diet and a way of life which will enhance health and survival.

A PARADOX: SURGICAL TREATMENT

In their desperation to obtain relief, undiagnosed CS victims will often grasp hold of any suggestion that offers to possibly provide help. Thus many have submitted to suggested surgical procedures which they and their surgeons have "hoped" would bring help. And strangely, for a brief time, the CS condition may become much improved after the surgery. The intestinal problems become quiescent and everyone is temporarily encouraged. Shortly their hopes are dashed to pieces when, all too soon, the disease manifests itself again in all its vengeance. How did it all work? What happened? The explanation is quite simple.

During the hospital stay the patient for several days (or longer) was kept on a light diet free from gluten-containing foods. Perhaps all food by mouth was eliminated as the patient was fed by intravenous infusions. With no intake of gluten the vulnerable intestinal linings were afforded an opportunity to begin to heal, hence the improvement in symptoms.

If patients and physicians would become more knowledgeable about the possibility of celiac sprue these unnecessary operations might become much fewer and these intestinal cripples would be better served. I say this not out of a desire to criticize, but merely to point out that we need to be alert to the possibility of CS whenever any patient presents strange symptoms which cannot readily be matched with a logical diagnosis.

Some children after tonsil surgery may experience similar CS remissions as far as their intestinal ailments are concerned. For several days they may subsist on little solid food and partake heavily of such non-gluten foods as Jello. The same mechanism of relief for their CS operates as with the abdominal surgery patients referred to above. The exclusion of gluten foods allows the gluten-damaged jejunum a period of rest and healing. Persons hospitalized for other medical reasons who have received many days of intravenous feedings have similar experiences. At least one such case is described later in this book.

When physicians note improvement in intestinal symptoms in a hospitalized patient they should properly ask the question, could this patient possibly have celiac sprue? Further testing is then indicated. Let us all learn to "think celiac sprue." Remember, there are multiplied thousands of such patients walking around out there, miserable and discouraged and sometimes depressed. Be alert for warning signs such as the ones we have noted herein.

DEPRESSION

Feelings of inadequacy and depression or discouragement are prominent features in adult CS cases that have not as yet been diagnosed and treated. When no one seems to understand the patient's feelings, or what to do to help them, the depression only deepens. Together with great physical weakness, memory loss and lack of concentration may be common.

One is almost shocked as one elicits a detailed medical history on adult CS patients to notice that so very many celiacs who were not diagnosed in their early stages have, because of the very nature of their affliction, suffered for years with feelings of depression and low self-respect. They may even express that they feel totally worthless, and they will have physical weakness to match their feelings. Family and friends too often do not appreciate the problem and sometimes offer "put down" criticisms which only serve to aggravate the patient's feelings of low self-respect.

Many of these celiacs in their early stages may not as yet have developed the severe diarrhea and flatulence symptoms that are so typical of more advanced cases of CS. Or they may have had severe constipation and may have reasoned that since maybe half of the population complains of constipation (judging from the burgeoning laxative sales), they should take laxatives. Others may spend a fortune on worthless colonic irrigations which are not a substitute for a proper diagnosis of CS. Thus everyone concerned who should be alert to CS is not "thinking celiac" and the person goes on undiagnosed and untreated. The depression only deepens.

Those who do have diarrhea might also be blind to that warning signal and credit it to "loose bowels" and try some of the various over-the-counter diarrhea medications.

Every week thousands of patients seek counsel from various practitioners for their feelings of depression and low self-esteem. Rarely do their counselors (many of whom are not physicians) suggest to their patients that maybe they should be checked for gluten intolerance. We have heard of many such detailed interviews and not once—we repeat, not once—have we heard or observed a counselor who would suggest a possible celiac sprue as a cause, or who advised an investigation of the intestinal tract as a root cause for the feelings of low self-worth or depression. Instead the patients are advised to have more psychological counselling and are given various tranquilizer types of drugs.

Surely among the multiplied thousands of such patients walking the streets of America there must be large numbers who are in their condition of discouragement because of celiac sprue. We cannot even guess how many, but when we finally see these patients in advanced stages of CS we (and they) wish that somehow in the early stages of their depression they could have been correctly diagnosed and managed.

Starts in Childhood

Since CS is a genetically mediated disease, the earliest symptoms probably began in infancy, with symptoms referrable to the gastro-intestinal tract. How important it is, then, that a careful childhood history be elicited in adult patients with obscure and puzzling complaints. Depression and low self-worth may become evident from early teen years and onward.

Further, if family adults are known to have CS, then it becomes imperative that parents be on the look-out for evidences of CS in their little ones so that if the genetic disease makes its appearance the condition can be managed very early— sparing the child a life-long crippling handicap with a severely damaged intestinal tract.

COMBATTING LOW SELF-RESPECT

If depression and feelings of worthlessness developing in cases of CS are allowed to continue, this will only make the bowel condition worse. Conversely, the worse the bowel distress, the worse the depression, and unless this cycle is broken each will constantly worsen the other.

Through constructive self-analysis without paying for expensive counselling services, just as the CS diet is a self-help program, so the patient needs to exert self-help for his depression and feelings of worthlessness. Counsel from someone informed on celiac problems might offer some help, but counsel from one not interested in CS problems and who might not identify the depression with CS could make the condition worse rather than bringing relief. Herewith we suggest a simple do-it-yourself program that can be modified and enlarged by the patient to suit his needs.

Ask yourself these pointed questions and write down your answers:

- Am I loving toward my family?
- Do I love my husband/wife?
- Even though I feel below par physically, do I have a desire to please and help others?
- Could there be others less fortunate than myself who are worthy of help?
- As I am able, would I wish to share my knowledge of the CS problem with others more needy than myself?

Scores of questions of the above type could no doubt be answered in the affirmative even by comparatively depressed celiacs, especially if they were given hope for relief by being placed on a total diet program.

Through dependence on divine strength that is God-given, all sick persons can reap benefits physically by endeavoring to be loving, kind and helpful to others at all times. Just as the condition of the body influences the mind, just so does the mental and spiritual condition give a "lift" to the body functions. It works both ways.

Mental depression and feelings of a lack in self-worth need not continue. In due time dietary reform should bring with it psychological improvement as the patient is willing to use his or her willpower to develop positive thought patterns. The chronic discouragement should lessen as the chronic intestinal process gradually improves.

Family members should assist by encouragement and by all means cease put-downs of the patient (if indeed, they have been guilty of this in the past).

Victory over depression and low self-respect can be expected. It may take time, but a sound program of diet and a rejuvenated mental attitude and outlook will do wonders in effecting the psychological re-education. Whatever the religious persuasion of the patient he should never forget that trust in divine power and help from heaven is a sure and ever-present source of encouragement and strength.

NUTRITIONAL HELP FOR THE DEPRESSED

Swedish investigators studied a group of celiacs who had been on a gluten-free diet for one year. (Hallert, C., Astrom, J., and Walan, A., "Reversal of Psycopathology in Adult Celiac Disease With Aid of Pyridoxine [vitamin B6]," *Scandinavian J. of Gastroenterology* 18: 299-304, 1983.) While their intestinal conditions had greatly improved, those who had feelings of depression reported no improvement. Then for six months 80 mg of pyridoxine was added to the daily gluten-free diet and the patients were re-evaluated: The symptoms of depression had abated.

Clearly, the depression experienced by many celiacs is at least partially the result of malabsorption and malnutrition. The findings of the Swedish researchers indicate that celiacs do need supplementary vitamins and minerals. I have a celiac patient who does much better by taking regular injections of the pyridoxine rather than by taking oral dosages as suggested by the Swedish researchers.

The nervous system and the voluntary muscular system may both become involved in CS to the extent that the disease must be differentiated from multiple sclerosis and also from myasthenia gravis, as well as other muscular dystrophies.

We have already noted that celiacs may be quite subject to mental depression, and of course, unless this is of a grave degree, it would be wrongful to treat such patients with the tranquilizing "happy pills" that are so commonly used to treat depression, unless the intestinal problem is given adequate consideration. It is most important to ascertain the true cause of the depression and if it is associated with CS the latter should be treated and managed hygienically with diet etc.

MUSCULAR WEAKNESS

Celiacs may develop numbness and tingling in the limbs and other portions of the body. One patient has described these as "sticking" sensations. In medical terminology they are called *paresthesias*. The confusing thing is that almost the identical sensations are produced in MS. These neurological manifestations may be a true part of the CS, or, as we show elsewhere, they may represent a concomitant presence of MS in the same patient. One disease can be an overlay on the other. As shown in the double-cousin primary families already reported, the two diseases may sometimes have a common hereditary connection.

I would not dare to claim that CS is the underlying cause of MS, yet the fact remains that in some instances CS may precede the evident development of MS.

Muscular weakness is a feature common to MS, MG and to CS. There may be a degree of muscular atrophy in all three. CS has been shown for at least 100 years to produce such profound muscular weakness in children that some have had trouble in walking and jumping like normal children. Weak children who plead with their elders to be carried instead of walking should be possibly suspected of having CS and should be carefully evaluated for celiac disease. In adult life weakness and atrophy is not uncommon in CS, to the extent that walking may become difficult and laborious.

SKIN RASH

One other nervous system condition associated with CS should be mentioned. It consists of a herpes-like skin rash on various parts of the body in CS cases and produces a very intense itching. It is persistent and aggravating. Treatment, other than symptomatic, is best directed toward correcting the diet program and eliminating gluten. Recovery may be slow. The condition is not in any way related to mouth or genital herpes. It merely gives a superficial resemblance to regular herpes infections. That is why it is called *dermatitis herpetiformis*.

MALABSORPTION

Incidental to the putrefaction of the intestinal contents, which is secondary to failure of proper digestion of the food mass, there is in CS severe hypermotility (diarrhea) as well as a failure of the intestinal lining to allow passage of nutrients into the bloodstream. Many nutrients are not yet prepared for digestion and absorption and many of these are frequently hurried out of the bowels in the hypermotility. As a consequence, the patient's nutritional state suffers.

Not only do some of the basic food nutrients become unavailable to the tissues through the malabsorption, but the vital minerals such as iron and calcium and also various trace minerals likewise become unavailable as they are lost in the rapid passage of the feces. It's the same with some essential vitamins. Calcium malabsorption can contribute to *osteomalacia*—a softening of the bones so typical in some cases of celiac sprue.

The impaired bowel walls also become unable to adequately transport (absorb) nutrients across the mucosal barrier and into the bloodstream. Fats in particular, especially the saturated fatty acids, are poorly absorbed in this failure.

NUTRITIONAL SUPPLEMENTS

It should be clear as day that any person with an active CS impairment of the intestines should be given supplementary vitamins and minerals. Because of the impaired absorption mechanism it is well to give some by injection, thus bypassing the impaired bowel mechanism. The B-complex vitamins can be given by injection under the guidance of a physician and the vitamin B12 is easy for the patient (or family) to give by injection. I recommend that CS patients be given 1000 micrograms (mcg) each week using one of the B12 analogs. Later the intervals can be stretched to two to four weeks for the injections.

B12 injectable is inexpensive, the syringes are inexpensive, and the injections are safe to give after a little instruction. Most patients can self-administer it. Some therapeutic purists will argue that the dosages are wasteful. My reply is, so what? No one can accurately tailor the dosage for each patient and with the material so inexpensive and so harmless, if a little more than is needed is given, is it not better that a little too much is given than not enough? It is not a toxic substance.

The most commonly used form of B12 is cyanocobalamine. Some authorities state their opinion that the hydroxy-cobalamine is better. I use both kinds. It is my experience that debilitated patients do better on injection dosages of B12 than to depend wholly on oral dosages, especially so when there is already a malabsorption problem in the small intestine in all patients with active celiac disease.

LACTOSE INTOLERANCE

The double sugars maltose, sucrose and lactose (milk sugar) are split into mono-saccharides (simple sugars) by their respective enzymes formulated in the "brush border" area along the tips of the intestinal villi, especially in the jejunum portion. Note the last syllable of each of the respective enzymes for the three kinds of sugars, which designates the substance as an enzyme. They are maltase, sucrase and lactase respectively. The sugars carry an O in the syllable; the enzymes an A.

Adults of many of the darker skinned races have by adulthood in most cases lost their lactase enzyme production and are no longer able to digest and utilize the milk sugar. A smaller percentage of lighter skinned adults of northern European origins may also lose their ability to digest and utilize lactose as food. In a few rare instances small children may lose this function also.

A few years ago, before the lack of lactose utilization by the darker races was understood, well-meaning American welfare sponsors shipped large quantities of surplus powdered milk to some of the Third World countries. They became perplexed when they learned that the recipients of their generosity did not consume the milk powder but instead (being frugal) used it to make "white wash" with which to white-wash their humble dwellings. Finally, the "generous" Americans realized that the lactose in the milk had made the natives ill and their seeming unthankfulness for the gifts received was only a way of putting the "unhelpful" gifts to some useful purpose.

The Mechanism of Lactose Intolerance

In CS, when the tips of the intestinal villi that are supposed to produce the lactase enzyme are damaged or destroyed, the lactase production is greatly reduced, or even eliminated. Thus the milk sugar in milk or milk products cannot be utilized. Then there is set in motion a chain of events approximately as follows: The lactose which cannot be split into simple sugars draws three times its own volume of fluid from the intestinal wall by osmotic action. Additionally, some of the lactose undergoes fermentation by bacterial action, producing lactic acid and gas and the intestinal lining is irritated.

All of these factors tend to increase the motility of the bowel causing the intestinal contents to be expelled in diarrhea. This added to the already voluminous intestinal contents and the usual diarrhetic stool so common in CS victims. Milk can be double trouble for celiacs.

In this entire process valuable minerals and electrolytes are lost as are also other nutrients. The milk products thus contribute to the malabsorption syndrome already present in the bowel of the celiac. (*Food and Nutrition Therapy,* by Krause and Mahan, W.B. Saunders Co., Philadelphia, PA, 1984, pp. 458-460.)

WHAT TO DO

Celiacs should not ordinarily use *any* *un*modified milk or milk products for the obvious reasons noted above. A few are able to tolerate soy bean milk, but so many celiacs have developed an allergy to soy milk and soy products that they cannot tolerate the substitute "milk." Additionally, soy milks may have added sugars either in the form of sucrose or malts made from barley and if enzymes for those sugars should be in short supply for the celiac, these sugars could induce a situation much like lactose intolerance.

There is now a remedy available for the lack of lactase activity in the bowel. A special bovine milk is available on many supermarket shelves called *Lactaid* (in a blue carton) wherein by treatment with lactase enzymes 70 percent of the lactose has been changed into the simple sugars. The consumer can reduce this to almost zero by adding eight to ten drops more of lactase (obtained in health food shops) thus making the milk almost totally free from the offending lactose and making it utilizable for celiacs.

Celiacs should *definitely* not use any milk or milk products that have not been treated.

Yogurt

Yogurt is said by some authorities (Kolars, *et al: New England Journal of Medicine* Jan. 5, 1984) to sometimes carry a smaller content of lactose for the reason that as the *Lactobacillus bulgaricus* and the *Streptococcus thermophilus* organisms which produce the yogurt from milk act upon the lactose converting some of it into simple sugars and lactic acid, the liability to produce lactose intolerance reactions in the bowel is reduced. This action is not total, however, and each celiac patient will need to be observant to see whether small amounts of yogurt can be tolerated in his individual case.

Sucrase Deficiency

Since the enzyme *sucrase* (which splits ordinary table sugar into two simple sugars) is also produced in the intestinal "brush border," it is logical to expect that there may be a degree of sucrose intolerance also present in celiacs who have sustained damage to their villi from the alpha-gliadin of the gluten. Accordingly, they would do well to avoid the use of sucrose in their diets including the sucrose of prepared foods. Simple sugars such as dextrose (corn sugar) or fructose, or even artificial sweeteners might be preferable to table sugar. Honey contains a mixture of sucrose and some simple sugars, therefore it might be slightly more preferable as a sweetener over a double sugar such as sucrose alone.

Should one use sucrose in the home canning of fruits? Yes, it can be used in moderation because in the long heating and boiling under the pressure of the sealed fruit jars, a substantial portion of the sucrose is hydrolyzed into one molecule each of dextrose and fructose (levulose)—simple sugars. Even so, it's best to use as little refined sugar as possible for reasons of sugar chemistry.

The B-Complex Vitamins

It order for the body to metabolize a given amount of sugar after absorption, a definite amount of a number of the B-complex vitamins must enter into chemical reactions as *co-enzymes*. Refined sugars contain none of these vitamins. Therefore, if the use of sugars is indulged, the body chemistry suffers from the lack of those vitamins and the result may be incomplete products of sugar metabolism. For example, it was shown years ago in experimental animals that pyruvic acid could accumulate in brain cells in the absence of a sufficient amount of some of these vitamins.

Let's remember that sugars are sugars, and no matter what kind is used, they all go through a similar chemical processing in the body. When used in their devitalized refined state we need to supply extra amounts of the B vitamins from other sources. We would all do well to limit the use of refined sugars. Celiacs have enough troubles as it is without adding sugar troubles to their metabolic load.

LACTOSE IN PILLS

Lactose (milk sugar) has for more than a century been used as a favorite binder, filler or extender in pills and capsules that carry medication, vitamins and minerals for patient use. It's a harmless sugar for healthy persons but for a celiac or someone otherwise intolerant to lactose it can be a very troublesome substance, initiating a typical lactose intolerance reaction.

Consider when lactose is used repeatedly during the day, day after day, how this insult to the intestinal villi in a celiac sufferer can add to an already disabling problem for CS patients. We have already covered this topic in connection with nystatin pills. Now we wish to stress to each celiac patient that you owe it to yourself to ascertain through writing to manufacturers of your pills to determine if your particular pill or capsule of medication of any kind contains lactose. Some bottle labels say, others will not. You need to find out for sure.

If there is lactose in your pills, you need to find out if possibly another brand will serve your needs better. To continue to use the lactose can only add to the problems of obtaining healing of the lining of your intestinal tract. If there is a medication that you cannot do without and it is not available in lactose-free form, you may still be able to take the pills if you supplement them with Lactaid lactase tablets. They will help to counteract the lactose sugar in the intestines.

The Lactaid corporation has prepared a booklet for physicians that lists more than 1,000 tablets and capsules that contain lactose. Their listing was obtained from data at the U.S. Food and Drug Administration through the mechanism of the Freedom of Information Act. Every celiac patient should have his list of pills and capsules checked from a list by his health care provider and if your pills are not on the list go direct to the manufacturer. The CSA/USA celiac association through its quarterly publication from time to time will list data on topics such as that which we are here discussing.

I have one of the booklets that lists the 1,000 medications. Every physician who advises CS patients should have a copy on hand to assist his patients. It can be obtained by him from Lactaid Inc.

If your physician does not have the booklet, ask him to obtain one so he can assist you in the matter. Patients may contact Lactaid Corp. directly for assistance in this matter also. See the Appendix.

3

WHEN CELIAC MEETS CANDIDA

Largely through the efforts of Drs. Orian Truss of Birmingham, Alabama and William Crook of Jackson, Tennessee the importance and wide distribution and incidence of intestinal yeast infections have become quite common knowledge, and thousands have been blessed by their research. The yeast involved is the Monilia yeast *Candida albicans*.

These pioneers in the cause of the yeast problem have shown in their publications how many chronically ill and misunderstood patients are yeast infection sufferers and their ministrations have brought relief and help to thousands—maybe millions of people—worldwide.

Candida can infect the mouth and indeed debilitated children may develop a condition called thrush wherein the yeast infection is easily visible in and around the mouth. Thousands of women suffer from yeast infections with discharge and itching in their vaginal areas. But the bulk of obscure yeast infections involves the intestinal tract where the complaints are more general and there is no easily visible lesion for the patient to see, or which the physician can readily see.

These yeast organisms are present almost everywhere and one

could almost wager that any intestinal tract, if cultured carefully, might be found to harbor the Candida organisms. But most of such cases would have no symptoms or complaints. It is when the yeasts begin to multiply enormously that they produce large quantities of toxins that can be absorbed into the system and begin to produce symptoms in distant organs (including the central nervous system), that intestinal yeasts create a problem that needs to be dealt with.

I believe in *some* cases (maybe even many cases) the presence of celiac sprue, which is secondary to gluten intolerance, offers a fertile substrate and culture medium for the propagation of the yeast organisms and that in any case of intestinal yeast infection the possibility of a concomitant CS should be considered until it can be confidently ruled out.

Rather than trying to write another book, I will recommend to readers Dr. William Crook's illustrated book *The Yeast Connection*, Professional Books, from P.O. Box 3494, Jackson, TN 38301.

These are typical symptoms of chronic intestinal yeast infections:

- Lethargy, feeling of being "drained"
- depression
- impaired memory
- numbness, tingling, or burning sensations
- muscle weakness or paralysis
- constipation and/or diarrhea
- severe flatulence
- mood swings
- general intestinal distress

Sufferers of CS and MS reading these lines will recognize some of the same symptoms in their own cases. Is there a possible connection? I believe there is.

A few years ago it became evident to me that at least *some* cases of digestive tract yeast infection were associated with CS and therapy for the CS resulted in improvement in the YI. Let us allow the following case report to illustrate:

One of my multiple sclerosis (MS) patients also had a severe diarrheal condition, so severe and intractable that a leading medical school faculty clinic diagnosed her as having Crohn's disease of the bowels and told her that it might become necessary to remove the entire colon, in order for her to survive.

At about the same time I had begun to investigate the use of the anti-fungal antibiotic, nystatin. I placed her on oral dosage. Much of her severe intestinal distress and diarrhea improved. At a later date when our therapeutic concepts had further matured and we realized that YI was often secondary to CS, we placed her on a gluten-free (GF) diet program and after a few months she was able to maintain reasonably comfortable bowel function on diet alone without the need for nystatin. The YI seemed be be completely controlled. In fact, it has now been several years since she has needed any nystatin at all to control any evidences of YI. This would strongly suggest that (in her case, at least) the underlying condition that permitted the YI to develop was the genetic defect of CS, and not primarily the YI itself. The YI was really a secondary problem.

It is of interest to note that the nystatin brought some improvement to her multiple sclerosis and the eventual switching to the GF diet for the CS brought even further relief to the MS, but did not of course "cure" the MS, which is a genetic problem as well as having other factors in the probable causation. This patient still (some years later) has some severe MS handicaps, including urinary bladder problems. But she is far less restricted in her mobility than she was before she undertook the GF diet program. Incidentally, she has all of these years, dating back before she used any nystatin or used the CS approach, been following the Swank low-fat diet regimen (described briefly in another essay) dove-tailing it with the CS gluten-free program.

How are CS and YI connected, if they are? I will briefly state my simple concept. The putrefactive processes in the bowels incidental to the maldigestion and malabsorption present as a result of the CS, furnishes in the intestinal contents an ideal culture medium for the propagation of the *Candida albicans* yeast organisms. A perfect, warm, moist and putrefactive environment—ideal for rapid multiplication of the yeasts.

Consider a simple household illustration: If a bruised apple begins to rot, what happens next? The decaying portion of the apple constitutes an ideal culture medium for molds and yeasts and they waste no time establishing themselves in the culture bed.

There are many fine treatment programs for yeast infections of the food tract and an appropriate diet program for the gluten intolerance experienced by genetically impaired persons suffering with celiac disease. But physicians often fail to recognize that there may be distinct interaction between CS and intestinal yeast infection. Actually, the CS makes chronic yeast infection possible by furnishing the habitat and culture medium for the Candida yeast.

PRACTICAL CONSIDERATIONS

There are millions of women suffering from vaginal *Candida albicans* yeast infection (YI). The standard treatment calls for the insertion of medications into the vagina. While this may help to suppress the infestation, it does not reach the source of the yeast problem. The genital infection is derived from the intestinal outlet located a scant inch or two away. To be effective, treatment must also be directed vigorously to the intestinal infection—the real source.

But that is not all. We have already called attention to the fact that most cases of intestinal yeast infection have an underlying process in the gut which furnishes an ideal culture medium for propagation of the Candida. Thus, patients with vaginal candidiasis need not only oral nystatin treatment for the food tract, but investigation as to their status in regard to gluten sensitivity. In many, many cases they need to be placed on a gluten-free diet. To do any less is to neglect needed treatment. In many cases, the mouth also needs local applications of nystatin powder. Many "sore" mouths and gums are simply chronic cases of candidiasis. (Dentists, please take note.)

One more suggestion: Acidophilus tablets or capsules may profitably be used in cases of CS and YI in early as well as later stages, as adjunct treatment.

The human intestinal tract is a very complex mechanism, designed to extract from ingested foods those nutrients that will best serve the welfare of the body. But the food must first be digested through various chemical reactions and prepared for absorption into the bloodstream.

The waste or surplus of food remnants are disposed of through fecal elimination. Most people probably imagine that human feces are mostly composed of such waste fibers. It's surprising, then, to learn that in many cases the greatest solid contents of feces is composed of bacteria that have grown in the bowels.

Intestinal Microorganisms

Candida yeasts are not the only organisms to inhabit the intestines.

A study conducted a few years ago and reported in a medical journal stated that they had been able to identify at least 400 different varieties of microorganisms living in human intestinal tracts. Not all of these are disease producers at all. Some may only be opportunists, but many also have a vital function in digestion and some of these internal bacteria (let's call them "friendly bacteria") are known to help produce vitamins from various foods residue, even vitamin B12, which is so essential to human health.

TREATMENT APPROACHES

Some clinicians treat primary intestinal yeast infection with antibiotics (like nystatin) and also limit carbohydrate foods (starches and sugars) in order to not "feed" the overgrowth of intestinal yeast organisms. So stringent is this restriction in some programs that patients are forbidden to eat fruits because they contain fruit sugar which would "feed" the yeast.

It is sad that so few of these patients receive that most important dietary counsel of all which is that they need to take a trial of a completely gluten-free diet to see if possibly by lessening the intestinal putrefaction of alpha-gliadin gluten foods they might thereby deny the culture medium and environment furnished by the putrefying food mass. Then the other dietary efforts and the use of the nystatin will really be effective and real progress is made.

In my experience, yeast patients need not give up of fruits and starches to effectively treat their condition. Reasonable quantities of fruits and unrefined starches may be used if the patient gives up gluten foods and takes nystatin orally. We need to keep in mind that it is the genetic defect of not being able to properly digest the alpha-gliadin gluten that permits its putrefaction in the intestines. This causes the malnourishment of these patients and also permits the yeast to flourish. All of this produces a constellation of symptoms that cannot be treated properly unless we reach the root cause. In many of these cases, the cause is celiac disease—gluten intolerance. From the complicated chemical mixup in the intestines, toxins from the putrefying foods and from the yeasts can be absorbed into the systemic blood circulation only to produce adverse and puzzling symptoms and effects in distant organs. Some of these toxins formed as a result of the gluten putrefaction are neurotoxins. They can adversely affect the nervous system and even aggravate various neourological conditions such as multiple sclerosis, for example.

In my clinical experience, celiacs who also take nystatin to control the yeast do much better than those who only follow the GF diet. Similarly, yeast infection patients who only diet by way of avoiding carbohydrates and take nystatin would do much better if they would eliminate the gluten-containing foods. At the very least, they should take the eating test and eliminate *all* gluten-containing foods for a few weeks. I predict that many will find they are much improved by taking this added step.

WHAT IS THE LESSON?

It is my considered opinion that every case of digestive tract YI might profitably be subjected to the GF diet test program, in addition to whatever type of antibiotic program is used. This may not be appropriate for every case, but one will never know if there is a CS connection or not, unless one investigates the possibility. And the test is not costly. It is self-administered as a home test, involving simple dietary changes, which, if in the end are found not to be applicable, need not be made permanent.

It is my experience that in the early stages of an obvious CS patient whose flatus and stools are so typical of CS, one might do well to consider several months at least of concomitant nystatin therapy to reduce the putrefactive toxic process of *Candida albicans* yeasts that are almost certain to be present in the putrefactive bowel contents. Surely every case of YI and every case of suspected CS deserves consideration of the issues raised in this chapter.

THE WONDER DRUGS

When I first entered upon the study of medicine we had none of the "wonder drugs" like the antibiotics. Many of our patients, despite careful surgery and medical management, would die right before our eyes. Croup claimed the lives of babies as we worked with them and performed tracheotomies to help them get a breath of air. Now all that is changed. We hardly ever see or hear of a grave case of infant croup. Antibiotics have saved millions of lives. They have been a great blessing.

But sometimes antibiotics may cause death and at other times when the life-saving drugs are given by mouth, they not only kill the streptococci and deadly staphylococci for which the drugs are given, but they will also kill off our "friendly" bacteria in the intestines. That is the risk we have to assume when we use oral antibiotics of the common types that deal with staph and strep types of germs.

Those same antibiotics also kill off some of the other "friendly" bacteria that tend to keep Candida yeasts in check and keep them from taking over the bacterial activities in the bowel. When these beneficial bacteria are killed by the penicillin etc., then the Candidas multiply enormously. Celiac sprue is not the only underlying cause of candidiasis. The overuse or abuse of antibiotics also is a contributory cause for the yeast development in some cases.

ENTER NYSTATIN

The intestinal yeast organisms cannot be controlled by the ordinary antibiotics, indeed, they have been the cause of some of the candidiasis episodes as we noted above. A few years ago someone developed a new antibiotic called nystatin which was quite specific for yeasts and various other molds.

What is more, though almost all antibiotics can be quite toxic in large doses when they absorb into the bloodstream, nystatin is hardly absorbed into the bloodstream—only in small percentages. Therefore it does not have opportunity to become toxic *systemically*. It does almost all of its work *locally* in the intestinal tract when given by mouth. So from that standpoint, although it is a powerful drug it is relatively safe. Of course, like any remedy, it should be used with care.

I recently had opportunity to peruse a list of about 1,000 prescription drugs supplied in a pamphlet compiled by the U.S. Food and Drug Administration. It lists all the drugs known to contain lactose, which milk sugar is used in many many pills and capsules as extenders and binders etc. It is ordinarily a harmless additive in medicine. But not for persons who suffer from lactose intolerance. Lo and behold, the listing stated that nystatin tablets contained lactose. That is probably a true statement as far as it applies to certain brands.

Happily there is a genertic form of nystatin tablets sold by a large drug firm in New Britain, Conneticut, the H.L. Moore Co. They sell nystatin tablets which their formulating company has certified to us do not contain any lactose or wheat. (They do contain corn as an excipient.) Thus they would be suitable for celiac sprue patients who tend to have lactose intolerance. The Moore Co. deals with physicians and drug stores. Your physician or druggist can secure lactose-free tablets for you from this company. (This statement about Moore is only made herein as a matter of information. I own no stock in the Moore company and receive no reward from them for this statement.)

The Lederle company makes available to druggists and physicians powdered forms of nystatin. This is preferred by many physicians over the tablet forms. I have used both kinds with my patients.

But drugs are not the magic potion for chronic yeast infection or celiac disease. Careful history, examination and diagnosis are essential. There must be a combination of diet adjustments with medications as indicated. And, since CS is a disease which produces profound nutritional deficiencies, careful and suitable dietary supplementations of vitamins and minerals must be carried out. Yet another medical name for celiac diseases is "Malabsorbtion Syndrome," so named because it produces an impairment to absorb good nutrients even if they have been properly digested. That's due to the handicap presented by the damaged jejunum section of the intestines.

The CS and YI patient must remember that her physician is only her helper. The patient herself must be the primary day-to-day manager of her own disease. This requires that she become knowledgeable of her condition. The principal reason I decided to compile this book was to help the patient to be all this, and to share with millions of CS sufferers what I have learned in my observations as a physician for over a half-century of medical practice.

4

CS AND MULTIPLE SCLEROSIS—A CONNECTION?

Perhaps the connection between celiac sprue and multiple sclerosis can best be illustrated by the following graphic case report:

In infancy and early childhood this female (now age 68) had severe digestive disturbances characterized by severe vomiting and diarrhea. The formal diagnosis back in those rural Utah times was "biliousness"—whatever that meant so many decades ago. (Incidentally, unexplained vomiting is common with CS children.)

As her teen years and early adult life developed she had fewer intestinal symptoms and maintained a tolerable, but at the same time a suboptimal, state of health. A lower back injury brought discomfort from time to time. Off and on ever since age 40 she has had attacks of bursitis in the shoulders.

SUDDEN INTESTINAL CRISIS

When she was in her late 40s an early stage adenoma of the uterus was discovered and was promptly treated with cobalt radiation and radical surgery. (There has been no tumor recurrence in the almost 20 years since then.) For a few years prior to the cancer episode she had had bouts of diarrhea with abdominal distention and increased intestinal gas, which all had been preceded by many years of constipation. Medical consultations over the years never suggested that celiac sprue should be considered as a diagnosis.

Within 36 hours after the first cobalt treatment to the abdomen and pelvis, violent diarrhea set in and lasted for many months. Despite the fact that the radiologists asserted that it was very unusual for cobalt treatments to adversely affect the bowels so very early, it was believed that the cobalt treatment must somehow have been the sole cause, strange as that would seem.

No one suggested the possibility of celiac sprue with superimposed aggravation from the cobalt irradiation. During the six-weeks duration of the radiation treatments she was placed on a very bland diet consisting largely of white bread, eggs, milk, applesauce and bananas. It was believed that these would be best tolerated. Little did anyone dream that the white bread (gluten food) and the milk (lactose) were really contraindicated for her damaged intestinal villi. It was years later—and a couple of major operations later—before her true celiac sprue would be diagnosed. No one suspected the presence of CS during the cancer and cobalt episode.

Intravenous Feedings

When the diarrhea became too severe to manage at home she was hospitalized and taken off all oral food. Feeding was strictly by continuous intravenous infusions, day and night. During these abstentions from oral food she would make remarkable improvement in her intestinal distress, but no one (not even her internist) tumbled to the idea that she could have CS.

Her troubles were all believed to be solely due to an unusual reaction to the cobalt treatments and as soon as the diarrhea cleared she was discharged from the hospital to resume the use of oral food. The diarrhea would soon return and she would be hospitalized again etc. She was going through the experience that so many celiacs have had. Eventually she survived the cobalt therapy and the radical hysterectomy and oophorectomy experience, but continued to suffer very poor health with almost daily diarrhea for about 10 years.

NEUROLOGICAL SYMPTOMS

Several years after the cancer surgery and cobalt treatments she developed neurological symptoms suggestive of MS. These included numbness, weakness, ataxia or poor coordination, loss of balance, double vision (diplopia), slapping foot gait etc. Several fine neurologists were consulted over a period of several years and numerous and exhaustive tests and studies were made. None would suggest either MS or CS even when her physician husband pointedly asked one of the neurologists, "Could she possibly have MS?" The prompt reply was a firm, "No."

Pains and numbness continued in the lower limbs. A podiatric surgeon even suggested excising a nerve from her foot to stifle the pain. The advice was not accepted but he did make an appliance for her shoe which gave no relief. When the lower limb distress continued, a fine orthopedic surgeon was consulted. He focused his attention on the destroyed lumbo-sacral disk, a residual from a back injury in early life, and advised a fusion operation to stabilize the joint.

The surgery was done and for a time the patient was encouraged but the neurological distress continued and the orthopedist advised that further investigation be undertaken of the peripheral nervous system. The neuromuscular deficits in the lower limbs continued.

Her husband who had for some time insisted that she had MS then said, "You are going to Portland [Oregon] to see Dr. Swank." (Roy L. Swank, M.D. of the University of Oregon School of Medicine, is probably the premier U.S. authority on multiple sclerosis.) Dr. Swank positively diagnosed MS, and her personal diet which already closely resembled Dr. Swank's low-fat diet was modified to bring it into closer conformity to his program.

Later this writer had learned of the research work of C. Orian Truss, M.D. of the University of Alabama in his treatment of cases of yeast infection with diet and the use of the anti-yeast antibiotic, nystatin. A keen observer, Dr. Truss had noted that some of his yeast patients who also happened to have MS reported some improvement in their MS while on the nystatin program for the yeast infection.

As we read the Truss reports we instituted nystatin therapy on our patient (and on several other MS patients also) even though this particular patient had no overt or obvious yeast-related symptoms such as vaginal infection. In fact she had *never* had any known vaginal yeast infection. Shortly after commencing the nystatin therapy, her diarrheal tendency was improved and the MS symptoms also improved for a period of two years, after which the improvement seemed to level off. The nystatin therapy was then discontinued.

About two years later severe diarrheal and flatulence episodes of a major nature began to recur. The flatulence was exceedingly foul. We finally suspected that she also had celiac sprue and placed her on a gluten-free (GF) diet program. Within 36 hours her most violent symptoms had almost totally cleared.

FINALLY, CELIAC SPRUE

In retrospect, we can now perceive that this patient had celiac disease since infancy which seemed to clear somewhat in early adult life, but was intermittently present in problems referable to the digestive tract. We now realize that her cobalt experience was that of a severe cobalt "burn" on an already damaged jejunum—the seat of celiac sprue. The cobalt would not have been damaging to a normal jejunum. The gross damage from the cobalt was more than the tissues could bear and heal and as long as she used gluten in her diet the jejunum continued to be damaged.

The multiple sclerosis (which was probably partially a genetic matter) also became evident in the midst of all these severe illnesses and all of them combined to make good medical specialists overlook things and evidences which now—in retrospect—seem so obvious. No criticisms of any are intended in these remarks. We're just being objective and this writer wishes his vision had been clearer during some of those years also.

Now, several years later, her MS has had its ups and downs and while her MS has gradually deteriorated it has been remarkably slowed. In some categories she is improved, in others not. But she is up and about every day and not every MS patient could sustain her activity so well for so long. Her CS diet problems are still with her as she searches for foods that are tolerated. More recently she has learned that lactose does not agree with her and elimination of it has helped her decidedly. Like so many celiacs she has developed a number of allergies to other foods such as tomato and soy products.

LESSONS

What are the lessons to be learned from this case?

1. There *is* some kind of connection between MS and CS in certain cases. Whether this is solely genetic or chemical in nature we cannot say. Since the discovery that she had both conditions, investigation of her two sisters reveals that they too each have MS and CS. They are all three offspring of one of the primary families described earlier. Both of the sisters have also responded to similar therapy.
2. There *is* some kind of relationship between intestinal yeast infection and CS, and also possibly between yeast infection and MS, although it's possible that the latter connection could be mediated via the CS connection.
3. If in her early adult years the significance of her intestinal history from infancy had been understood, perhaps she

could have been spared years of later distress. Had the GF diet been adopted many years earlier, perhaps her present intestinal health would have been almost normal. Perhaps, too, the MS would never have become the major problem that it has. Yes, a detailed history, clear back into infancy, can be important.

4. Multiple clinical problems can complicate the making of a diagnosis. In this case the old back injury, undiagnosed celiac disease, and the MS, created a puzzle that was difficult to sort out. The uterine cancer with the cobalt therapy added yet another dimension to the puzzle. Clinicians and patients alike need to learn to "think celiac sprue" and to "think multiple sclerosis" whenever a patient presents puzzling problems involving either the intestinal tract, or the peripheral nervous system, or both. Not that we should eagerly hang CS and MS diagnoses on people willy-nilly, but we must ever be conscious that these conditions (which generate so many obscure symptoms) must be kept in mind much more than usual and thus spare some of our patients years of distress and sickness.

5. There is much that we do not as yet understand about the relationships between CS and MS. Much additional study is needed. If this writer has seemed dogmatic in some conclusions, it hasn't been out of a desire to claim definitive knowledge, but rather to stimulate readers (whether lay or professional) to think deeply on these perplexing problems and to share observations.

The experience of the reported case can in some ways be duplicated in one of the readers of this book. Twenty-four years ago it was established that she had MS. Her mother, plus five of her 11 siblings, also had MS as did several cousins and two of her own five children. Is there a genetic connection in MS? Draw your own conclusions from all these cases.

The 64-year-old lady with MS for 24 years finally developed severe diarrhea and she was placed on a gluten-free diet. In 48 hours the severe symptoms disappeared and are now controlled by the diet. Without question, for all of these many years, the gluten sensitivity has been an adverse factor in her MS problem. Once again we document the fact that in some cases there *is* a connection between MS and CS. We are constantly learning of more and more similar cases.

DIAGNOSING MULTIPLE SCLEROSIS

That fine medical specialists can find it difficult to arrive at a diagnosis of multiple sclerosis (MS) has been amply demonstrated. Despite many theories as to causation, MS is a disease of unknown cause wherein the myelin sheaths, the fatty substance which surrounds nerve fibers like insulation, become dissolved, thus hampering transmission of nerve impulses.

At the risk of seeming to be overly simplistic, for lay readers we might liken the picture to electrical wires which have sustained loss or injury to their covering insulation and this permits a "short-circuiting" of the electrical impulses.

MS produces a host of diverse neurological manifestations, including numbness, weakness, paralysis, tingling and burning sensations (paresthesias), loss of balance, poor coordination (ataxia) with a difficulty in walking, and impaired and double vision are common early signs.

Bladder and bowel control may become impaired and impotence and libido loss are common. A spin-off of many of these personal disturbances is that family relationships may be disrupted and the divorce rate amongst couples where one partner has MS is greater than that of the general population. Sometimes mental and emotional imbalance may be evident when the MS patient comes under stress. Both the patient and the spouse need to learn to control their feelings and actions and be supportive of each other.

The sample symptoms mentioned above may be found in various combinations in various patients, depending upon which set of neurons (nerve fibers) happens to be involved in the disease process. The nerves involving the lower extremities seem to be more frequently involved than those of the upper extremities. The face and even the mouth and tongue may be the location of MS disabilities. Speech may also be affected.

Because the symptoms and impairments experienced by MS patients depend upon which specific nerves are predominantly involved, it's difficult to formulate a specific list of "classical" MS symptoms and findings which can always be depended upon to ensure an accurate and early diagnosis of MS. Therefore, typically, many MS patients suffer obscure symptoms and distress for years before a definitive diagnosis can be made. Many physicians seem hesitant to tell a patient, "You have MS," for fear of frightening and discouraging the patient: as though they were giving the patient a final sentence consigning him to a life of doom in a nursing home and wheelchair.

This fear is unfounded, for as we have shown herein, there is much that can be done to help MS victims with diet and other modalities so that they can live useful and satisfying lives. That is *if* they are reached early enough in the development of the disease.

To procrastinate in recognizing MS and to be afraid to utter the words "multiple sclerosis" and to put off the day of reckoning by placing the patient on tranquilizer pills to assuage the vague and troubling complaints experienced by the patient, only delays the opportunity for the patient to receive needed help. As we have mentioned before, some of these patients are referred for psychotherapy when they could be better helped with diet therapy. Thus much valuable treatment time is lost.

THE SWANK PROGRAM

In the 1940s Roy Swank, M.D. (professor of Neurology at University of Oregon medical school) discovered that a high fat diet (especially of saturated fats) impeded blood flow to vital organs and he devised a low-fat diet program for his many MS patients. His diet has been eminently successful in bringing about many remissions and slowing down the progression of the ravages of the degenerative processes of MS.

In his *Swank MS Newsletter* for December 1987, Dr. Swank tells how he developed the concept of limiting dietary fat intake to 20 grams per day, most of which should be in the form of oil fats—unsaturated fats belonging to those classes which contain the essential fatty acids.

Since dietary fat is essential in order to maintain health it was very sad to note the fad that passed through some circles a few years ago wherein some "nutritionists" declared that 10 percent fat was all one needed to remain in health. The fad turned out to be a disaster for some persons, especially for some with MS. Happily the no-oil fad did not last long, although we still hear of persons who follow it. One of my MS patients tried it for six weeks and the MS condition worsened remarkably but recovery came when oil fats were reintroduced into the diet. Anther person on that program also wrote to us for counsel having had a health setback from the "no-oil" fad.

Needless to say, I know from clinical observations that the Swank diet program is meritorious and rather than trying to give all the details in this volume I shall urge interested persons to contact his office at Department of Neurology, 3181 SW Sam Jackson Park Rd., Portland, Oregon and make inquiry about the availability of his diet book and his newsletter.

A CS Connection?

Having already shown that at least in some MS cases there is a definite CS connection, I wish to suggest to MS patients that they might wish to consider combining the Swank diet principles with the gluten-free program for enhanced results. If the patient has CS as well as MS, such as some patients I have described, then the combination would prove beneficial. A trial of this self-help idea is surely worthwhile and could bring gratifying results. If not, the gluten foods could simply be re-incorporated into the diet.

Incidentally, Dr. Swank believes that, "MS patients have a

metabolic defect which prevents them from being able to utilize saturated fats in a normal way." Sounds a little like the fat malabsorption problem experienced by CS patients, does it not? Yes, there may be some kind of connection between CS and MS.

Admittedly, the diagnosing of MS is not always a simple matter and the case reports we have noted show how readily MS can be overlooked. In citing these cases it is not with intent to be critical, but only to urge diligence in recognition of the early signs of MS and CS also. The only absolute way to diagnose MS is at autopsy, but this is not a very viable option for the living to accept. More recently some sophisticated imaging machines have been developed which it is said can demonstrate graphically MS lesions in the brain.

Dr. Roy Swank believes that 95 percent of these cases can be diagnosed in life and he has available a blood test to assist in this process, thus making an earlier detection possible than if we should have to depend solely on general clinical findings.

VISUAL DISTURBANCES IN MULTIPLE SCLEROSIS

A member of one of the primary families reported earlier in this book experienced episodes when her vision would fade out for a week or more and then return. She resided in another state and her visits with us were infrequent. Examination of her eyes when her eyes were not troubling her would yield no positive clues, for at those visits she would not be experiencing fade-outs.

In her home community she sought help from physicians and even ophthalmologists, but no definitive diagnosis was made. MS was never mentioned to her. One practitioner advised her to consult a psychiatrist, who in turn gave some very strange and inappropriate counsel.

However, on one occasion she visited me purposely because she was having blind spots and fade-outs of the vision and in my examination I was able to demonstrate the blind spots in the retina of her eyes. It was then that I made the diagnosis on the basis of the history, the retinal blind spots and other neurological signs. I told her plainly that she had multiple sclerosis and referred her to Dr. Roy Swank who concurred in the diagnosis.

She is the same patient discussed elsewhere who had been diagnosed as having Crohn's disease. But we have been able to obtain relief for her with the use of nystatin and later she was further helped by taking up the GF diet program. Thus, like her two sisters, she had both MS and CS.

An Early Sign

A rather sudden and unexpected loss of vision, especially in a younger person, can occasionally be an early sign of MS. Indeed, many decades ago it was well known that an inflammation of the optic nerve where it enters the eye (referred to as retrobulbar neuritis) can be one of the early signs of MS.

Some MS patients may have sudden blanking out of a part or all of the vision of one or both eyes without any apparent reason for the episode. The event may represent a transient circulatory impediment in the flow of blood to the retina or nerve of the eye. The event may last only a few minutes or sometimes for days. Any patient who has such attacks and who has not been diagnosed as having MS should certainly be carefully examined to see if possibly he or she does have MS.

Because these "blanking-out" episodes are so intermittent and transitory, they pose a real difficulty in relating them to MS in the early stages of the disease. This is also true with double vision. The latter can come from various causes other than MS, and is a prominent feature in myasthenia gravis also. If physicians will keep in mind MS as well as the myasthenia when these symptoms present themselves, perhaps many of these patients might be diagnosed in their earlier stages.

ANOTHER CASE OF MS AND CS

In the early 1950s the well-known British playwright, Rodger MacDougall, was diagnosed as having multiple sclerosis. But as too often happened then, his physicians kept the diagnosis from him. (This is a practice that we have noted from time to time and all the while the disease progresses and valuable treatment time is lost.)

MacDougall became a helpless invalid, confined to bed and wheelchair, but when he finally learned that he had MS he set about doing something about it, more or less all by himself.

By study and trial and error he adopted what we would now call a celiac sprue dietary program, free from all gluten. He also excluded all milk products and free sugars and ate freely of fruits and vegetables. He also excluded most animal fats and depended more on seed oil fats—much like the Swank diet program. In fact, we could consider his program to be a combination of the best of the CS diet with the best of the Swank diet. He formulated his own vitamin and mineral supplements to take the place of those excluded by his restricted diet.

Astounding Results

In due time the bedridden actor was able on his diet to attain a remission of his MS and was eventually able to be up and about as physically active as anyone his age. We have seen a photo of him practically jumping. Eventually he wrote a book about his experiences.

Do I believe that there can be a CS-MS connection? This case would suggest as much, especially when added to the cases I have reported herein. MacDougall's exclusion of dairy products is suggestive of the similar exclusion forced on many CS patients because of their added lactose intolerance.

A Postscript

The patient described earlier in this book a few years ago happened to borrow a copy of the MacDougall book from a friend. She decided to try his "wheat-free" ideas on her own MS condition. For some reason she was not impressed with the rest of his program and continued to use rye, barley and oats. Nevertheless even by excluding the principal gluten grain, wheat, she was able to enjoy six weeks of improved health as far as MS symptoms were concerned. But then she suddenly began to have aggravated intestinal symptoms and then gave up the whole program and went back to her wheat.

In retrospect, what had happened was probably this: having excluded wheat with its heavy gluten content, she was greatly benefited in her as-yet-undiagnosed celiac sprue, and the gluten intake diminution brought benefits to her known MS. Still in retrospect, in order to satisfy her craving for bread, she then loaded up heavily on the other three gluten grains which she should have excluded together with the wheat. In the end her efforts were self-defeating. Now, years later, she wishes and wishes that she had gone all the way on the MacDougall diet program which she is now basically on, not because of the MacDougall book, but through a better understanding of the pathologic physiology of her CS and MS.

Could there be others out there who have CS or MS, or both, who might be wise to consider MacDougall's account and the story we have related? We think so. CS and MS have some things in common; more research is needed.

5

GLUTEN AND HYPERTENSION

This is a medical detective story that may come as a complete surprise to most of our readers. It is of course well known that incidental to the debility and below-par physical state of most CS patients many of them suffer from *low* blood pressure. This is also true of many persons with various forms of allergy. These facts are not anything new.

But have you ever imagined that perhaps elevated blood pressure (hypertension) might be associated with a case of celiac sprue, so closely associated that the eating of a gluten food like wheat will elevate the pressure markedly?

THE DISCOVERY CASE

About 24 years ago a case of seriously and persistently elevated blood pressure came to my attention, and I found that if the patient ate wheat the blood pressure would elevate markedly and if wheat was excluded the pressure would tend to become normal with a systolic pressure of 120 mm. Hg.

One evening when the patient's pressure was normal he

indulged in two slices of wheat bread and a small amount of fruit for supper. By midnight he was awakened with a pulsating headache; his head felt larger than a basketball and the systolic pressure had risen from 120 to 230, high enough to be able to precipitate a stroke. But he quickly took some strong blood pressure pills and brought the pressure down to a manageable level.

At another time a similar test sent the systolic pressure up to 180. Even this level has been known to sometimes produce a brain hemorrhage and stroke. During the months when all this was going on the patient noted considerable looseness of and "growling" in the bowels. We did not associate these symptoms with a possible CS. We assumed that this was a case of true allergy to wheat.

Research

A careful research of the *then* current medical literature brought only silence on the question of food idiosyncrasy (allergy) and elevated BP. But when I dug into older medical journals, back into the 1930s, I found several well-documented research papers reporting an aggregate of 40 cases of vascular hypertension which could be shown to be due to "allergy" to foods, mostly to wheat. Elimination of the wheat from the diets had brought relief of the elevated blood pressure.

Why had not medical science caught up with the discovery and adopted diet control for hypertension? It just so happened that at about the same time some efficient drugs became available that would lower the blood pressure and with drugs being so much more simple to manage (but not necessarily better) than diet therapy it appears that physicians in general forgot about the natural diet remedy and went all out for the drug program.

COLOSSAL PROBLEM

The magnitude of the hypertension problem in America is so great that there simply are not enough doctors and clinics to efficiently manage the possibly 40 millions—yes, millions—of Americans who suffer from significantly elevated blood pressure. One writer described how, if all those patients were ordered on any given day to seek medical help, the traffic would jam every highway and every medical facility and bring the country to a standstill. The theoretical illustration, though impossible, does illustrate the magnitude of the problem.

How many of these cases are associated with dietary factors we cannot say, except we know there must be vast numbers of them. Interestingly, while I was still in active medical practice and we skin-tested many patients for allergies, we found that of those who tested positive to wheat, many of them also had some elevation of the blood pressure in comparison to those who did not show any allergy to wheat.

To alert the public to the fact that there could be dietary factors in the causation of elevated blood pressure I later wrote my book *Drop Your Blood Pressure,* which was published and circulated by the tens of thousands by Pyramid Books of New York. (It is now out of print.) In the book I set forth the results of my research and studies.

At that time my concept was that the mechanism was strictly one of outright allergy, the wheat antigen stimulating an antibody reaction in the body, and that the elevated vascular pressure was somehow secondary to the allergy and the allergens. Now, however, I have some second thoughts. Could there be some kind of relationship to celiac sprue?

A Gluten Connection?

Since the time that I reported the "discovery case" in my book it has become evident that that patient, who is still alive, now shows distinct evidence of having celiac sprue. While much of his reaction to wheat did appear to be a straight antigen-antibody reaction, there are in retrospect other features which point straight to celiac sprue. I now have begun to wonder if the 40 cases reported in the medical literature in the 1930s were simply wheat allergy or did at least some of the patients have celiac sprue. There is no way of checking that out. But the discovery case definitely meets the clinical criteria for CS.

I relate these personal observations in order to raise the question of whether or not investigators in the field of celiac sprue might not need to consider that *some* cases of vascular hypertension might possibly be associated with celiac sprue, the latter contributing to a causation of the elevated blood pressure, all this in spite of the fact that many celiacs do have a low blood pressure. Obviously much research needs to be done. In the meantime we need to keep these matters in mind.

I know of a man who has hypertension and has suffered a severe coronary heart attack secondarily. He is a heavy eater of wheat. He is not my patient, but I cannot help wonder if his blood pressure would not drop to better levels if he tried a GF diet for a few weeks. Surely it would not hurt if a few thousands of the severe hypertensives in America would try a GF diet for a while. It might be very revealing.

Earlier, we cited estimates by authorities that there are maybe a million celiacs in North America, many of them yet hidden. Just think what it would do to the guesses and statistics if even a small percentage of the hypertensives could be shown to have celiac disease as a contributing cause! It would surely upset the statistics. In the meantime we must wait for brave researchers; those courageous enough to begin to think on these things and do some investigating.

There is an old saying that "one swallow does not make a summer." Likewise, one celiac whose hypertension can be shown to be substantially affected by his celiac sprue does not prove that the connection is widespread and common. I plead for research!

6

MYASTHENIA GRAVIS AND CELIAC SPRUE

Myasthenia gravis (MG), like CS and MS, is a disease involving the immune system and seems to be genetically mediated. Its true prevalence is not great, nevertheless the national MG association in its radio advertising urging people to become aware of this muscular dystrophy disease makes the public statement that "This year 100,000 new cases" can be expected to surface.

THE NATURE OF THE DISEASE

In brief, the disease is more common in women, but men over 50 also are affected. The onset may be unexpected without warning; the first evidences may be such things as muscular weakness of the vocal organs, or the swallowing mechanism, or the external eye muscles that move the eyeballs, producing double vision. I know of one patient whose first inkling was when he swallowed some vitamin pills as was his custom and one ended up in his lung. All voluntary muscles are likely to be affected.

The active lesion is that of a "blockage" where the nerve fibers connect to the muscle fibers. The result is that nerve impulses do not "come through." There is an insufficiency of the neurotransmitter chemical acetylcholine that fails to be produced at the point of synapse between nerve and muscle. Some kind of deranged immune response is the culprit that destroys some of the receptor mechanism at the neuromuscular junction. Since some muscle fibers cannot be stimulated to contract, the fibers in due time atrophy. All this results in shrinkage of the muscle mass and continuing weakness.

TREATMENT

Until recent decades mortality from this autoimmune disease could reach 30 to 40 percent, but since better treatment with drugs and better understanding of the pathophysiology this mortality figure has been markedly reduced. Yet it was only a very few years ago that a well-known international person died of the disease.

However, the drugs (such as Mestinon and Prostigmine) only help control the symptoms. They do not reach the cause of the disease. Other treatments include removal of the thymus gland in the center of the chest, behind the breast bone. This formidable operation is believed to help some patients. The thymus gland being a part of the immune system does seem to play some kind of part in the causation of MG. MG also responds favorably to the use of cortisone type drugs as does MS and even CS, but naturally cortisone is not the ultimate long-term treatment of choice. I say again, these drugs do not effect a cure.

A RELATIONSHIP TO GLUTEN INTOLERANCE?

I report here the case of a 60-year-old man whose MG came on so gradually that a pill he was swallowing ended up in the lung. Several times after that the same "accident" almost happened.

X-ray studies confirmed the fact that the swallowing mechanism malfunctioned on the right side of his throat. A well-known neurologist confirmed the clinical diagnosis of MG. Regular dosages of Prostigmine for the past ten years have controlled some of the muscular weakness by facilitating nerve impulse passage at the neuromuscular junction.

By now readers of this volume, dealing principally with celiac sprue, may wonder why this single case report is being inserted into this monograph. Here is the reason: Since the discovery of the MG in this patient it has become evident that he is also gluten intolerant and in the past few years since the GF diet has been followed carefully, the MG, while still present, has actually shown some improvement. This is why I feel constrained to report this case.

We've already shown that there is some kind of connection between CS and MS. Is there also a connection between gluten intolerance and myasthenia gravis? We do not have the answer. We hope lay persons and professionals alike will be alert to this possibility as suggested by this single case.

Let us not laugh at a single observation. Many a scientific discovery has grown from a single observation that has been duly reported to others. If this is simply an oddity and a happenstance, well, we can learn that too, if others will be observing.

Addendum

Since the first writing of this book, we've been consulted by a patient who read the book and exclaimed, "It's the story of my life." She suffered from myasthenia gravis, having had the condition for years. Her mother died of the disease and she has a sister who also has the affliction.

But here is the interesting point: It is evident that she also suffers from celiac disease. So, now we have observed *two* cases of this association. Is there a connection? There surely could be. We naturally wonder how many more such associated cases are wandering around out there only half diagnosed. Wherever there is gluten intolerance associated with MG, the latter can be benefited by dietary management of the gluten problem.

7

ASSOCIATED AUTOIMMUNE DISORDERS

Readers should really read Dr. Ann Lawrence's chapter 20 in the book *Living With Celiac Sprue*, published by the CSA/USA. It tells an all-too-common story of how even in a medical family the presence of celiac sprue can be overlooked.

But the portion we wish to focus on is her assertion that rheumatic fever seems to be very frequent in cases with CS. She relates case after case. Could it be that diseases of the joints and ligaments can be common in CS patients? She comes to the conclusion that a number of autoimmune diseases (of which the rheumatoid types of diseases are examples) "exist on the same chromosome. Sprue is also on this chromosome." (p. 188) There we have it. If this concept which was published years ago is still valid, this may explain why a number of diseases seemingly unrelated to sprue do nevertheless seem to have some kind of connection.

Rheumatoid Disorders

There are a number of joint and ligament and muscle diseases that have a commonality in that they are related to autoimmune disorders. They include various kinds of arthritis (including rheumatoid arthritis), polymyositis (multiple muscle stiffness and pain), bursitis (of the shoulder region), just to name a few. If these have their genetic code "sitting" on the same chromosome as that of CS, is it any wonder that these rheumatic types of disorders are seen in CS cases?

In reviewing family histories on reported cases of CS in medical literature one is impressed how often rheumatoid arthritis comes up, as in the cases mentioned by Dr. Lawrence. In one of the primary families reported earlier the mother of the three female CS cases had very severe and disabling rheumatoid arthritis since the age of 21, lasting of course until her death at age 59. There is no way of knowing whether she also had CS, but one of her daughters in reviewing her problems is almost certain (in retrospect) that she must have suffered with celiac sprue. During the last two years of her life she had much diarrheal disease.

Of her three CS daughters, two had rheumatic fever in their 20s. One of these now in her 50s has arthritis of hands and the one in her 60s has had shoulder bursitis since her 40s.

A male celiac of our knowledge has all his life been afflicted with tendencies to joint and muscle pains and in his old age has considerable spinal osteoarthritis. He's also had many bouts with shoulder bursitis requiring repeated injections of cortisone-type drugs when the pain and stiffness becomes too severe to bear.

Another more recent female patient with CS complains of much morning stiffness and pain in joints, also some swelling.

We must conclude from such evidences as we have cited that it would not be correct to assume that there was not some kind of connection between CS and the various "rheumatoid" types of joint and connective tissue diseases.

Since self-help testing for gluten intolerance is so exceedingly simple if done properly, we must conclude that it might be profitable for persons with these other autoimmune diseases to test themselves for a few weeks on the GF diet to see if there could be a connection inasmuch as some of these conditions carry genes that "sit" on the same chromosomes as do the genetic markers for CS. (Dr. Lawrence.)

Even if the CS does not "cause" the bursitis or arthritis, or whatever, at least if the patient's health and well-being can be enhanced by controlling a CS condition, at least the general health and well-being of the patient should rub off to some benefit for the rheumatic condition.

Surely CS patients and their physicians owe it to sufferers of some of the "other" autoimmune disorders to begin to "think celiac" and be alert to signs and symptoms of CS and thereby bring blessings and help at least to a few sufferers who otherwise might go through life in below-par health and wonder why.

THE TRUE INCIDENCE OF CELIAC SPRUE

Early in this book we considered how many celiacs there were in North America—according to expert authorities. No one really knows, but maybe the questions we've raised will suggest that the true incidence is much higher than we have ever dreamed it would be.

There are no truly accurate figures for the incidence of CS in the general population. Even in Great Britain, where many studies have been made, there are fluctuations in the various figures collected. There also seem to be fluctuations in incidence between wartime and peacetime, which may represent variations in the amount of wheat eaten, according to some investigators. American "estimates" (and that is what they are, "estimates") vary between 100,000 and one million. When prodded, authorities admit that the estimates may be too low.

We have shown herein that some MS patients also have CS. If large numbers of MS sufferers could be tested for CS one wonders if they would swell the statistics of CS. We have also raised the question whether certain patients who are gluten intolerant and who also have elevated blood pressures that are affected by their wheat intake might also affect the statistics if a representative group could be studied. Perhaps it is time for many patients and clinicians dealing with these other diseases to become celiac conscious.

If anyone wishes to challenge my suggestion that maybe the true incidence of CS is much higher than is generally believed, *then hear this:*

I have personal knowledge of a small rather rural church congregation numbering about 45 adult members wherein five white adults definitely have celiac sprue. That would be about 11 percent. None of these five persons are blood related and all have come from various geographic regions. Thus there are no common genetic or environmental factors operating.

Additionally, one member (not among the five above, and not related) died with a gastric cancer several years ago. But even before his cancer became evident he had some classical symptoms of CS, such as uncontrollable and foul flatus, and an intolerance for wheat. His personal physician apparently never suspected celiac sprue. One of the five persons above has a 3-year-old male child who had only had one formed stool all his life. From dietetic experimentation the mother suspects that possibly both of her children may be showing signs of having celiac disease. However these children are not counted in the 11 percent noted above.

One more point of interest. There is a summer visitor to the little church (but not a local member) who also has celiac sprue and intestinal yeast infection. She follows the GF diet and also has used nystatin for extended periods. She too is not counted in the 11 percent. It may interest readers that in this congregation with so many celiacs a deaconess whose husband has CS furnishes gluten-free communion wafers for the use of the CS patients in communion services four times yearly.

In no way do I suggest that we should extrapolate the 11 percent incidence in this church sample to the general population, but I agree with some of the CSA/USA members who've expressed the opinion that most estimates for CS incidence are too low. None of us knows the real figure.

Does any reader wish to stress that the five cases I mention constitute an exceedingly small sample? I would fully agree. But allow me to point out that without one medically oriented family in the congregation being alert to the diagnostic criteria for celiac sprue, perhaps not a single case of the five would have by this date been diagnosed as having CS, maybe not even suspected of CS.

One wonders how many other population groups might be similarly situated. For the reason that no one in their midst is CS "oriented" people simply continue vague distresses and illnesses and no one seems the wiser. Even in the tiny sample group which we mention, none of the remaining 40 adults have been clinically checked for CS. It was just that the five cases developed so much difficulty that the medically oriented family could advise them that CS must be considered in their cases. The CS diet brought proof.

Is it not safe to conclude that people, laymen and physicians alike, all need to become alert to the evidence of celiac sprue?

A Postscript

One wonders how many patients with intestinal yeast infection also have celiac sprue. If these were added to the statistics, think of the totals that might result! No one knows for sure. Yes, yeast patients also need to "Think celiac" and do some diet testing.

Since the first writing of this book yet another patient with celiac disease happens to be affiliating himself with the small church congregation. Thus the percentage incidence is raised another point or two.

Surely all of these facts point to a vast incidence of celiac disease, far more vast than the experts can imagine.

We've shown that certain gluten foods are "enemy foods" for persons with celiac disease. They are likewise "enemy foods" for some persons with multiple sclerosis and also for victims of intestinal yeast infections, at least in some instances. In all three of these diseases the immune system of the body is involved.

But what about a host of other autoimmune diseases where the body's immune system is definitely compromised? Think of the various forms of rheumatic and arthritic disease, a host of allergies, lupus erythematosus etc. Then there is psoriasis, that terrible skin affliction for which there is no known cure. We don't even have a clear understanding of its cause.

The Heartbreak Disease

Psoriasis, with its extensive scaling over raw, inflamed skin, has been aptly called the "Heartbreak Disease." Heartbreaking for the reason that it can be so incapacitating with little hope for relief, and cures so difficult to find.

Not long ago I received a letter from a dear friend who is terribly afflicted with psoriasis, pleading for help and asking if there was possibly anything new to suggest. Yes, there is something new to suggest—at least for some of the sufferers. I know of one celiac who had some annoying psoriatic patches on his arms that have largely cleared since the gluten-free diet has been carefully followed.

What's more, the book *Fighting Disease* (Rodale Press, 1984) cites a French experiment wherein "Eleven people with stubborn and severe psoriasis who were gluten intolerant" showed "remarkable improvement" and "less frequent relapses" when placed on GF diets.

Surely every psoriatic should try the GF diet program, but let me stress once more that the GF diet test may be valueless if the subject does not go all the way and meticulously exclude *every* tiny morsel of food related to any and all of the offending gluten foods. Plus, the test should be continued for quite a number of weeks in such a stubborn disease such as psoriasis. Relief should not be expected in just a few hours.

ARTHRITIS

Arthritis often accompanies psoriasis. Danish researchers (cited in *Fighting Disease*) found that oral zinc sulfate definitely benefited cases of psoriatic arthritis. Really, persons with any kind of arthritis need to consider the possibility of gluten intolerance and "think celiac" at least long enough to try the GF program for a time. The program will not benefit all arthritics, but the test is so simple and costs nothing but a little effort and perseverance.

There are so many diseases that are poorly understood and for which we have no specific treatment. Some of these will improve under cortisone treatment, but that cannot be the final answer. Could it be that a careful diet analysis and a test diet would reveal some enemy foods? It may not always be gluten. We'll never know if there are enemy foods in any given case if we don't try to find them.

DOUBLE SADNESS

But it's so sad that so very few, even among those who suffer from debilitating diseases, are willing to even try any test diets—even for a few days or few weeks—to see if possibly a change in diet might prove helpful and bring some relief to their affliction and chronic suffering. People are so skeptical. Appetite and taste have a stranglehold on many individuals.

A second sadness is that so few professionals seem interested in advocating diet analysis and test diets. They readily order laboratory tests but such tests, while valuable, do have their limitations.

The most definitive test in diagnosing celiac sprue is the "eating test," considered, of course, in the light of the history and other physical findings. I feel certain an eating test, of whatever nature to be developed, could prove helpful in other disease syndromes also. We never know until we try.

8

DOWN'S SYNDROME, DEMENTIA AND SCHIZOPHRENIA

IS CELIAC DISEASE A PARTNER?

Some scientists suspect there is some kind of a link between certain forms of mental illness or retardation and celiac sprue, but the research is just beginning and the topic is highly controversial.

However, the theories are worth considering and the test—the simple gluten-elimination eating test—may well be worth the two- or three-week trial it takes to see if you or your family member improves. It certainly can't hurt! Consider this gluten-free food for thought.

DOWN'S SYNDROME

Down's Syndrome (DS) is a genetic birth abnormality which occurs in about 1:700 live births. Infants from mothers over 40 years of age may be born in a frequency of 1:40 live births. The genetic defect is situated on chromosome #21 and at birth these children usually have 47 chromosomes instead of the normal 46.

The infants suffer from weakness, misshaped small heads and mental deficiencies. Most do well to have an IQ of about 50. Many die at a young age but some live on into middle life of 30s and 40s. General development is much slower than that of normal children. The facial appearance is Mongoloid and for that reason the condition is often referred to as mongolism. Other congenital defects and skeletal deformities are not regarded with surprise in these cases. There has been no treatment of value for these patients except to provide good custodial and nutritive care in order to make the best of a disappointing situation.

An interesting observation has been made by many investigators, namely, that patients with Alzheimer's disease (AD), sometimes called senile dementia, usually have genetic abnormalities and, as in cases of DS, the abnormal genes are believed to sit on chromosome 21. Naturally this has raised questions such as, are AD and DS in any way related? It is a fact that of those DS individuals who live until in 30s or 40s the incidence of AD is greater than it is in the general population. We believe these facts to be significant.

In the March 20, 1987 issue of the *Journal of the American Medical Association,* we find a very authoritative article by Harold Mozar, M.D. and his associates dealing with the causative factors in AD. Dr. Mozar is in charge of the Alzheimer's disease program for the California State Department of Health. In this article which explores all of the extant theories and findings on AD it is stated very clearly that:

> Almost all individuals with DS who live beyond the age of
> 40 years develop typical Alzheimer's lesions. Comparable
> pathologic features extend to immunologic impairments and,
> in Down Syndrome with dementia, to cortical cholinergic
> defects.

The writers then go on to state that even the amino acid sequences of amyloid fibrils in the degenerated brain tissues of both conditions are in general identical and that AD and DS are in some way genetically linked on chromosome 21. They further supply the hypothesis that there may be a virus that helps to initiate both AD and DS in genetically suitable individuals. (It's a well-known fact that other immune disorders with central nervous system abnormalities such as multiple sclerosis have been suspected by many investigators to possibly be precipitated by viral mediation, provided the genetic impairment is already present.)

NEWS FROM AUSTRALIA

An Australian physician, Chris Reading, together with associates, has over a period of years in his medical practice carefully evaluated the family histories of more than 2,000 patients. Among many of his discoveries as to genetic facts he discovered that out of 18 children with DS, 17 positively had gluten intolerance and in the remaining case he was suspecting the same in that child also.

In his recent book *Your Family Tree Connection* (Keats Publishing, Inc., New Canaan, Conn.) he describes his most interesting "medical detective work" and his findings in many other diseases besides DS. But what is most fascinating about his studies is that he found that by placing the DS children on a gluten-free diet fortified with various vitamins and minerals he reported concerning the DS children as follows on page 202 of his book that they "have made rapid and measurable improvements in height, head circumference, weight, mental and motor development and general health."

Having observed that these children seemed to be deficient in various minerals and vitamins, and knowing that persons with gluten intolerance all have a malabsorption problem with nutrients, Dr. Reading fortified their diets with formulations featuring vitamins B1, B3 (niacin), B12 and various minerals, particularly zinc.

Certainly if I had a Down's Syndrome child in my family I would not hesitate to investigate whether or not the child also had celiac disease and if there was *any* chance that he did I would certainly place him on the Reading diet program. There could be much to gain and nothing to lose, even if the program didn't help the child. There surely could be no harm in any given case of Down's Syndrome in investigating the possibility of there being a concomitant presence of celiac disease.

I recently saw an infant with a clearcut DS, whose father has gluten intolerance and whose mother had a close direct antecedent who had Alzheimer's disease. The three facts which we have enumerated surely strongly suggest that the Reading findings may have validity. I advised the mother that the child should be investigated for gluten idiosyncrasy. Hopefully the child could be benefited by a gluten-free diet and possibly, years down the road, perhaps AD development could be averted. Many DS adults develop AD. Various figures are given by investigators. One figure which I have heard was 85 percent. I am sure some figures might be lower.

TREATMENT CONSIDERATIONS

In past decades treatment of Down's Syndrome has consisted mostly in good custodial care and general diet plus such limited education as could be arranged for. Over the years many DS children have from birth or infancy been placed in institutions for the feeble-minded as a sort of warehousing therapy while waiting for the child to die. In recent years more humane approaches have surfaced and there are now training programs where physically and mentally defective youngsters are being taught many skills, enough in some cases so they can be self-sustaining.

Currently it may be fashionable to advise that these infants be given vitamins and minerals to enhance general nutrition. But, if Dr. Reading's findings can be substantiated, these children should *all* be tested for gluten intolerance and if any is found they should be placed upon a gluten-free program. In fact, it would be well for the mother to also be tested. We don't know yet if any gluten-derived toxins might be transmitted in breast milk to an infant.

ALZHEIMER'S DISEASE

It was a spring day in 1967 and my dear life companion lay dying in a university hospital of an inoperable brain tumor. I had learned that she would pass away before another day would end. As I walked down the hospital corridor I met up with an aged medical college professor, a very kind and godly man. He did what he could to assuage my grief, and give me sympathy.

Then he briefly shared with me his own family problem. His wife of many years lay helpless in a nursing home, and then he added, "She does not even know me when I visit her." She was afflicted with Alzheimer's disease, a progressive brain degeneration with dementia. I quickly realized that while my impending loss, which took place within hours, would be great, his loss in some ways was even more hard to bear, for he was living through the experience of a "living death."

His wife was for all practical reasons intellectually brain dead and there was nothing medical that could relieve her situation. She would continue to suffer on, and so would he. At least in my wife's case, her suffering would soon end and then in due time I could begin to think about how to order my future life. This experience shared with me by my old professor gave me a close glimpse of what millions of U.S. families experience day by day as the mental faculties of their loved ones seem to drain away little by little.

What Is Alzheimer's?

Alzheimer's disease can be defined as a progressively degenerative brain disorder that may become evident as early as the fifth decade of life or as late as the tenth decade.

Aged individuals may also develop dementias from other causes associated with arterial hardening, brain hemorrhages and a succession of strokes. Sometimes it may be difficult to distinguish between the two forms of dementia noted above, or indeed, the same person could suffer from both kinds at the same time. A recent medical journal article pointed out that head injuries sometimes predisposed victims to AD and in it cited that a number of well-known retired boxers developed AD in greater proportion than the general population. (*Journal of the American Medical Association*, May 12, 1989.)

A Genetic Problem

Many studies have demonstrated that AD is also a genetic problem and in this present decade scientists have located the defective predisposing gene as being situated on chromosome #21, which happens to be the same chromosome upon which the defective DS gene resides. This may be very significant.

There is yet another environmental factor which has for many years been proposed as playing a causative role in Alzheimer's disease: It is aluminum. Time and again, researchers have seemingly disproved the hypothesis and time and again someone comes up with new evidence that seems to implicate aluminum in the causation of AD. As of now the matter is not settled.

A re-activation of this theory finds support in the British medical journal *The Lancet* for April 8, 1989. Therein one writer calls attention to the affinity of aluminum for the nuclei of nerve cells. It has also been demonstrated that brain tissue of AD patients carries a much higher level of aluminum than normal brains. Yet another *Lancet* reporter calls attention to the fact that hot water heating tanks often have aluminum electrodes in them and the metal gradually dissolves in the water, causing the householders to ingest the aluminum in their food supply. A similar dissolving of aluminum can take place in aluminum coffee pots. Have you had your daily dose of aluminum in your coffee today?

Yet another possible source of ingested aluminum is the common use of aluminum hydroxide in some of the highly advertized antacid stomach remedy pills and liquids. We must not forget to mention that pickles are often treated with alum astringent (aluminum sulfate) and some baking powders also contain alum. Too much aluminum can be toxic as has been shown in accumulations in the blood in patients undergoing kidney dialysis therapy.

Memory

Loss of memory is often the earliest symptom in cases developing AD. Forgetfulness is common. If any medical treatment is to be beneficial it will have to be given in the early stages. In the later stages there is too much actual brain tissue destruction. No treatment can restore the jumbled nerve fibers and debris to produce functioning nerve cells. Basically and tragically, there is no real treatment for any advanced case of Alzheimer's except general custodial care.

Early Cases

Dr. Reading of Australia holds out hope that maybe nutritional therapy and a gluten-free diet might be helpful even as it is in Down's Syndrome cases. He bases these concepts on the relationships between the two diseases: Both are genetic diseases and both have a defective gene resting on chromosome 21. Also, DS persons who live to middle life are more prone to develop AD than are normal persons. Thus theoretically, if diet therapy helps DS, it might also help AD. Since Alzheimer's disease tendencies tend to run in families it would certainly be prudent for anyone who had close AD relatives to be tested for gluten intolerance and if positive to place themselves on a gluten-free diet program together with suitable vitamins and minerals. The concept operates on the assumption that it could be a "preventive treatment" for persons who "might" be possible candidates for future AD. This statement is clearly speculative.

All that can be offered for possible Alzheimer's disease therapy is early diagnosis, good general diet, a trial on a gluten-free program purely on a theoretical basis since such therapy seems to be beneficial in Down Syndrome patients.

If we can rightly depend on the DS-AD relationship it should be obvious that anyone with gluten intolerance would be wise to diligently follow the GF diet in the hope that maybe, just maybe, the onset of Alzheimer's might be possibly averted or delayed. As of now this is clearly a theoretic statement, but it might turn out to contain some wisdom. Considering the hopelessness ahead for the average AD sufferer and their families our suggestion might be worthy of consideration.

NEW RESEARCH

Scientists are constantly on the prowl for possible causative factors and new treatments for AD. One researcher claims to have good results with anti-coagulant medications. He claims improvement in early cases.

Since there is a lack of the neurotransmitter chemical acetylcholine in the brains of AD patients, when the substance is administered into body tissues it is unable to pass the blood-brain barrier. One researcher has conceived the idea of installing a small plastic tube into the brain cavities and regular doses of acetylcholine are then injected through this means. He claims good results in early cases. But this is heroic therapy and technically difficult. I would doubt that this will turn out to be the treatment of choice, but it certainly will help in the study of AD. Some have suggested that the ingestion of capsules of lecithin and choline might help the brain in the synthesis of the deficient neurotransmitter, but thus far this has not proved to be dependable therapy.

It has been known for many years that persons in various stages of senility can be benefited by exercise, and without question exercise would be beneficial for AD patients, though not curative. Anything which quickens the flow of blood to the impaired brains should be helpful.

On the basis of possible association with DS and gluten intolerance, certainly all Alzheimer's patients should be screened for possible gluten problems and treated with a GF diet if indicated. I would say that if I had an AD case in my family I would deem it worthwhile to empirically place such a person on a GF diet for several months as a trial to see if any benefit could accrue. *It cannot do any harm* to make such a therapeutic trial, even though we must admit that it is wholly empirical.

Now it is quite fashionable to readily suspect Alzheimer's disease in any oldster with mental and memory lapses. In Alzheimer's disease there is actual primary tissue degeneration. Not every case of senility with memory failure should be considered as having Alzheimer's.

As pointed out by Dr. Arthur C. Walsh in his book *Conquering Senility*, various circulatory and hormonal causes can also produce dementing effects and on page 35 of his book he mentions vitamin B12 deficiency as one of the causes of senile dementia. We have already pointed out that yet another B-vitamin deficiency, namely pellagra, can produce dementia, a dementia which can be reversed upon the institution of a proper diet.

In the aged, impaired blood circulation due to arterial hardening is the norm. Obesity also contributes to such circulatory problems. Lack of vigorous exercise also impairs brain circulation resulting in sludging of the blood in the vessels. This deprives nerve centers of a vigorous blood supply.

In advanced cases of Alzheimer's disease the brain tissue shrinkage can be demonstrated on various scanning and imaging films, but not so in the early cases. Accordingly, early cases of senile mental abberations and memory failure can only be presumptively considered as Alzheimer's cases and in many instances they are not Alzheimer's disease at all.

Therefore, every case of inordinate memory failure and other manifestations suggesting Alzheimer's should have the benefit of nutritional fortification, even if done empirically. This would include all the B vitamins and injections of B12. Niacin tablets have proven helpful in the aged with memory problems. It functions by dilating the smaller arteries, thus bringing nourishing blood to the vital brain centers.

We urge that *every* suspected early case of Alzheimer's disease be treated nutritionally and at the same time it might be worthwhile to consider the use of a gluten-free diet.

If one waits until brain atrophy becomes so severe that it can be demonstrated by imaging films, one has waited too long to apply helpful therapy. Such a delay is comparable to the delay that many multiple sclerosis patients suffer when physicians are loath to make the diagnosis until the patient is either bedridden in a nursing home or at least confined to a wheelchair. The diagnosis should be made early while beneficial therapy can be instituted.

That "chemical" substances elaborated from the interaction between gluten and the intestinal lining can enter the bloodstream and exert toxic effects on distant organs is well estab-

lished. That some of these substances can be psychoactive or
psychodepressive we believe can also be established.

Earlier we have recorded our observations to show that the
avoidance of gluten contact can have a beneficial effect on the
symptoms of multiple sclerosis, at least in some cases. We are forced
to the conclusion that the exclusion of alpha-gliadin gluten from
the diet prevents the formation of neuro-toxic substances in the
alimentary tract, thus preventing such toxins from having adverse
effects upon the already demyelinated neurons. We do not know
the chemical nature of these particular neurotoxins.

It is likewise well established that dermatitis herpetiformis represents a toxic reaction to neurotoxic substances associated with
gluten ingestion in celiacs. The skin patches of this peculiar
dermatitis produce intense and persistent itching, unrelieved by
the usual anti-allergy and anti-pruritic medications. The only
effective treatment in most cases seems to be careful elimination
of dietary gluten over a period of months (or years in some cases).

We have in this volume recorded preliminary observations which
suggest that gluten intolerance may be a factor in aggravating myasthenia gravis which is an immune system neural derangement wherein the transfer of nerve impulses from the nerve ending to the
muscle cell is inhibited owing to a lack of neurotransmitter chemicals. We must assume that some kind of neurotoxin is responsible
for producing this interference at the neuromuscular interface.

As pointed out, mental depression can be a prominent feature
in untreated cases of celiac disease. It is this writer's opinion
that this fact is not simply a reflection of emotional discouragement but may in fact be the result of neurotoxins exerting a
psychodepressive effect directly upon the mind. We have no way
of absolutely proving that such toxins can pass the blood-brain
barrier and produce depression, but there are many general
diseases that can produce toxins that can depress mind functions
and mental alertness. Why not gluten idiosyncrasy as well?

Some Case Studies

If further studies can duplicate Dr. Reading's findings (in 18
cases) that Down Syndrome patients almost universally suffer

from gluten intolerance and that when a GF diet is instituted considerable improvement in health occurs in neurophysiological findings, then we must conclude that reaction between the gluten and the intestinal lining liberated neurotoxic substances which adversely affected the brain and nerve cells of those DS patients who consumed gluten foods.

DS patients are born with considerable neural deficits. The fact that their neural functions improve when gluten is excluded from the diet suggests indeed that some kind of neurotoxin has thereby either been kept from forming, or has been removed, or has been neutralized. The exact nature of these neurotoxins is not known. We also wish to stress that the Reading studies have not as yet been duplicated in the U.S.

But, would neurotoxins such as we have suggested be exclusively harmful only to neural tissues such as the already damaged brains of DS patients? We hardly think so. A neurotoxin could as easily affect an unimpaired brain. But such effects might not be as easily noticeable on an unimpaired brain as on DS cells. That the foregoing assumptions may be reasonable can be illustrated by the case report which follows.

PSYCHOACTIVE TOXIN?

The father of this patient has furnished to us the following facts: Between the ages of 15 and 18 the young lady began to gradually exhibit psychotic and personality changes. Finally hallucinations, delusions and paranoia surfaced. Continuing consultations and search for possible reasons for the mental abberrations in this otherwise intelligent person were fruitless until a nutritionally oriented psychiatrist suspected possible celiac disease. Gluten was promptly excluded from the diet.

Six weeks on a wheat-free diet eliminated almost every abnormal symptom. The young lady is now 32 years of age, a normal, highly intelligent, practicing attorney.

Her father, a professor of psychology in a large college, describes her present status as follows: "To this day, she cannot eat anything with gluten in it three days in a row without beginning to hear voices."

One cannot but wonder how many, many persons diagnosed by some as genuinely psychotic may in reality be suffering from the effects of neurotoxins that can be effectively eliminated by simply excluding all gluten-containing foods. Would that not be much more physiologic and desirable than plying these patients with various mind-altering and mind-depressing drugs and tranquilizers? Perhaps more psychiatrists should begin to study nutrition. The one who diagnosed this case surely did.

SCHIZOPHRENIA

For many years the cause of schizophrenia was shrouded in mystery. But a few decades ago it became evident that altered brain chemistry was involved and then followed suitable drugs that could modify the chemistry. A number of investigators have now demonstrated that diet and nutrition can be definite factors in causing the disease. In the Fall 1986 issue of *Clinical Ecology*, Beatrice Trum Hunter has made an extensive review of the literature on the topic. Here are some of her findings:

> Is gluten intolerance related to schizophrenia? Dohan [Dr. F. Curtis Dohan of the Medical College of Pennsylvania] thinks that it is. He has been studying the biochemical associations with schizophrenia. As early as 1966, he reported four observations:
>
> 1. Children with celiac disease, more often than by mere chance, became schizophrenic adults.
> 2. Psychoses occur in adult celiacs more often than by mere chance.
> 3. Gluten can induce common behavioral disturbances in both children and adults who are celiacs, and these disturbances subside after introduction of a gluten-free diet.
> 4. Often, during times of psychic stress or acute infection, the severity of celiac disease symptoms increases. In some instances, this is accompanied by an increased severity of schizophrenic symptoms.

Dohan suggested that in gluten-intolerant individuals, gluten may enter the brain and affect the nerve receptor sites. Peptides from gliadin may be the neuroactive substances that go from gut to brain. Dohan's subsequent studies strengthened his original observations. *

About ten years after Dohan's initial report, M.M. Singh and S.R. Kay of the Bronx Psychiatric Center studied schizophrenics who had been improved under neuroleptic drug therapy and who were on cereal grain-free diets. When adding gluten foods they noted that the patients regressed in their improvement and after removing the gluten challenge they would improve again. Suitable control cases were maintained. They concluded that there were schizophrenia promoting properties in the wheat gluten. (Their findings were reported in *Science* magazine 191:401-402, 1976.)

Other studies have also demonstrated that where gluten-containing grains are freely used, such areas have a higher incidence of celiac disease than other areas which are similar except for a lower use of the cereals.

Other Neurotoxins

That other neurotoxins can under some circumstances produce psychotic behavior is evident from this case. A young woman suffered violent psychotic disturbances. The cause was finally traced to heavy metal poisoning (mercury amalgam) in her dental fillings. Complete relief was not obtained until the offending heavy metals were excised from her teeth.

Earlier in this century, before white flour had its depleted vitamin content restored with added vitamins of the B complex, pellagra was not uncommon in certain U.S. regions where white bread and devitalized corn were staple articles of diet. Many of these pellagrins developed psychosis so severe that they were committed to mental hospitals. After it was discovered that pellagra was primarily a manifestation of an avitamin-

* (Dohan, F.C. Cereals and schizophrenia: data and hypothesis, *Acta Psychiatr. Scand.* 42:125-52, 1966.)

osis (i.e., vitamin deficiency) and the patients were given the proper B vitamins and a better diet, their dementia disappeared and they could be discharged from the hospitals. Cases of pellagra are now exceedingly rare.

It's quite possible that the toxic effects on the brain cells in the pellagrins were not purely the lack of vitamins, per se. Without question there must have been neurotoxins also involved, these being developed by the avitaminosis B. About 70 years ago James S. McLester, M.D. showed in animal experiments that actual nerve cell degeneration could take place when B vitamins were lacking. Such substances as pyruvic acid were shown to accumulate in the blood and also in the brain and heart tissues and exert a toxic effect. Over 40 years ago I commented on this research in my book *Science and Modern Manna*. These facts were well understood over a half century ago. In the matter of the pellagra cases it is clear that the psychosis-producing substances (toxins) were elaborated in the body through faulty chemistry associated with the avitaminosis.

I cite one more observation relative to neural damage in gluten intolerance. The malabsorption of nutrients that takes place in celiac disease results in varying degrees of malnutrition. Lack of vitamin B12 may cause degenerative changes in neurons and regular B12 injections help improve neural function in many diseases, including celiac sprue.

We have no present way of estimating the magnitude of the relationship between celiac sprue and severe neural malfunction. However, I fear the association could be of an enormous magnitude.

Nor do we understand why neurotoxins attack certain portions of one person's body and other portions in another body. Perhaps the toxins find weak "chinks" in the genetic makeup, or the immune system/protective "armor" and thus concentrate their force on these susceptible locations.

One thing is certain: We need many more astute neurologists, psychologists and psychiatrists to "think celiac" and investigate the nutritional status of their patients—all of them.

9

YOUR IMMUNE SYSTEM TO THE RESCUE

SUPPORT FOR THE IMMUNE SYSTEM

Since in celiac disease and also in MS, MG, and chronic yeast infections the immune system is usually impaired there will be times when added support should be supplied for the immune powers. I have found it exceedingly valuable to provide this added help for my CS and MS patients.

In blood plasma there is a protein fraction that has the power to help fight off infections. It is gamma globulin. For clinical use it is extracted from healthy, pooled human plasma and when injected *intramuscularly* it strengthens the immune powers of the recipient blood to help overcome infections through natural mechanisms. Other debilitating conditions also seem to be benefited.

Candidiasis patients who sustain an injury or infection requiring the use of broad-spectrum antibiotics know that the latter will aggravate their condition. Therefore this therapy may be eminently helpful to lessen, or maybe even to obviate, the need for antibiotics.

(Readers may wonder, could the modern plague, AIDS, be transmitted through the use of gamma globulin since it is made from human blood? Medical authorities assure us that, besides being produced from the blood of screened donors, the extracting and processing is such that the gamma globulin is *totally free* from any AIDS viruses. It is supplied in sterile vials ready for injection as needed.)

Dosage and Administration

An average mild infection may require only a single 2.5 cc. dose of gamma globulin given intramuscularly, with great care to test that the needle point has not entered a vein. More severe infections may require 5 cc. and may need several days of repeated dosages. Gamma globulin is relatively inexpensive, but must be given under the order and supervision of a physician. However, nonmedical persons can be instructed to administer it safely. Some of my patients have learned to give it to themselves.

You should not be surprised if your family doctor has not heard of the concept of using gamma globulin in the management of these immune system diseases which we have been discussing. He may be better acquainted with its use in such conditions as infectious hepatitis. But my experience indicates that this substance has a much wider field of usefulness. In cases of flu it is eminently helpful in ameliorating the infection and in reducing the fever.

In Multiple Sclerosis

Researchers in the field of MS have found that some patients are benefited by intravenous infusions of human plasma from healthy donors. This usually requires a little time as the patient receives the slow infusion in a medical office or hospital.

Since the gamma globulin is extracted from pooled human blood plasma its effect can be considered to be very similar to that of the infused plasma, but in this case it's administered as an intramuscular injection requiring one minute.

Since I have found gamma globulin to be so helpful in some MS patients who also have celiac disease, I am also studying the usefulness of injections for cases of CS who do not have

MS. After all, both diseases have much in common and both involve the immune system.

Gamma globulin is not a harmful substance. It's not a "drug" in the strict sense of the word. It's truly a natural remedy, a physiological modality that simply enhances the natural body defenses.

I've never noted an adverse reaction or intolerance to it. Of course, it's possible for any therapeutic substance to somehow produce an allergic reaction under special circumstances. But I've never encountered one in the hundreds of injections given by me or under my supervision.

Your family doctor might appreciate knowing of the usefulness of gamma globulin in immune disorders.

Encouraging benefit is sometimes obtained in multiple sclerosis patients by the intravenous infusion of blood plasma obtained from blood banks. Usually this requires that the patient have this done in a physician's office or as an outpatient in a hospital setting.

Somewhat similar beneficial results may be obtained by the intramuscular injection of several cubic centimeters of gamma globulin, which does not require a medical office or hospital stay of an hour or two. It can be accomplished as an office visit or even in the home. Some patients feel much better if they take an injection about once each week for a period of time. As mentioned earlier, it seems to support the functions of the immune system of the patient.

In several chapters dealing with a number of immune system disorders we've recommended vitamin B12 injections as a supplement. Readers may wonder how we propose to "connect" B12 with these diseases.

AN ESSENTIAL NUTRIENT

Vitamin B12 is universally recognized as an essential nutrient to aid in such functions as the manufacture of blood cells, in the function of digestion and in the metabolism and function of cells of the nervous system. B12 is not a single chemical substance, but rather a name for a number of *corroid* substances, all of them distantly similar to portions of the hemoglobin molecule of human blood cells and also somewhat resembling the chlorophyll molecule of plants. In man, an atom of cobalt occupies the center of the B12 molecule.

The vitamin is intimately related to cell enzyme systems and to such specialized functions as the proper development of red blood cells. Indeed, it is in its latter relationship in anemia prevention that the vitamin has evoked such great interest, and it has also been so much misunderstood. So many scientists have over the years jumped to unwarranted conclusions regarding food sources of B12. But while its relationship to anemia prevention has received the greatest public attention, its relationship to the nervous system is equally important.

Cyanocobalamine is the official name given to the most commonly used form of corroid in clinical and hospital practice. Hydroxycobalamine is yet another form preferred by some physicians. In the cyanocobalamine there is an atom of cyanide in the vitamin molecule. But it is not in a toxic form of cyanide and can be used freely.

Nerve Cells

B12 is a factor which helps produce and maintain the myelin sheath insulation around nerve fibers. Loss of the myelin and degeneration of this sheath is a well-known feature of multiple sclerosis. Without an intact myelin sheath, nerve impulse transmission may be seriously impaired.

A veritable potpourri of neuropsychiatric symptoms can present themselves in cases of B12 deficiency. Subtle mental changes, loss of balance, numbness, tingling, weakness, and even depression can be outstanding symptoms and memory loss may be prominent. A mixture of a number of the above may lead patients to simply feel "below par" with no clear-cut indications that would lead the casual thinker to identify it all with B12 deficiency.

We should mention one more astounding observation. Almost 40 years ago a New York investigator first reported cases of incontinence due to B12 lack. The list keeps on growing. Not only do we all need to "think celiac." We also need to be alert and "think B12." Think of a possible deficiency.

NUTRITIONAL SUPPLEMENTS

Incidence of B12 Deficiency

No one knows the true incidence of B12 deficiency. Dr. Robert Allen and associates at the University of Colorado studied 323 cases of deficiency and found that more than half (141) evidenced nerve damage and of these, 40 had no evidence of blood abnormalities such as would lead one to suspect B12 deficiency. (*New England Journal of Medicine*, June 30, 1988.)

Similarly, a study by Dr. Ralph Carnel of the University of Southern Calif., (*Archives of Internal Medicine*, Aug. 1988), reported that 33 percent of 70 patients with deficiency revealed *no* blood abnormalities. The author also stated concerning B12 deficiency that, "The experience at our hospital suggests that deficiency is more common than is currently appreciated."

A Harvard university study concluded that "a lot of cases of B12 deficiency were missed" because of technical problems in the chemical testing for deficiency. We cannot always place full faith in the laboratory tess.

In many immune system disorders (some of which we have already discussed) there may be a host of obscure symptoms and findings that involve the central nervous system and many of these can be associated with B12 deficiency. Keep in mind that clinical evaluation is as important as the laboratory tests.

B12 and Viruses

Some astounding research with bacteria which may have human implications and value came out of the University of Virginia about 15 years ago. The scientists found that bacteria deficient in B12 would permit viruses and other destructive factors to enter the bacterial cell and to destroy it. (*Infectious Diseases*, May 1974.) Yet another bit of research, this time from England, has shown that in B12 deficiency conditions certain vital tissue enzymes will not be formed, and essential substances are not able to enter body cells. (*Lancet*, June 22, 1974). So here we have cited evidences that in B12 deficiency states vital substances cannot enter living cells, whereas destructive substances and viruses are able to enter. Conversely, in the presence of adequate B12 levels, vital substances find ready entrance, while viruses may be denied entrance

The implications are clear. Perhaps when a virus infection strikes, we should not only think about loading up on vitamin C but also take some extra vitamin B12. I can't promise it will help, but it just might and certainly will do no harm.

As a final word on the role of viruses, we shouldn't forget that it's believed that viruses may at least be inciting factors in triggering underlying genetic problems. One prime example of such would be multiple sclerosis. The viral connection hasn't been proven, but has often been cited as a possibility by experts in the field. If it should prove to be a valid concept, consider how helpful correction of a B12 deficiency might prove to be. Let's also keep in mind that viruses have also been postulated to be factors in activating Alzheimer's and celiac disease.

Many years ago the eminent nutritionists Michael G. Wohl, M.D. and Robert S. Goodhart, M.D. emphasized that if adequate supplies of the B-complex vitamin pantothenic acid are present in the tissues less B12 is required (*Modern Nutrition in Health and Disease*, Philadelphia, Lea and Febiger, 1955, p. 407.) The pantothenic acid seems to exert a "sparing" effect upon the B12, reducing the total requirement for it. They also cite a number of authorities who have demonstrated that when the B vitamin riboflavin is present in high concentration, the synthesis of B12 is facilitated in the body. (Some authorities describe such synthesis as taking place in the intestinal tract through the mediation of intestinal bacteria.) Certain portions of the chemical formulas of B12 and riboflavin have features in common.

Why a Deficiency?

Adequate amounts of dietary B12 are found in most animal foods (meats, milk and eggs). In spite of this, those who suffer from B12 deficiency are most commonly those who eat animal foods.

Pure vegetarians can also become deficient, but contrary to popular medical opinion there *are* non-animal sources of dietary B12 in a vegetarian diet program.

Since B12 deficiency only rarely occurs because of an absolute lack of the vitamin in the diet, we must look elsewhere for the reasons for the deficiency. We find the reason in the lack of, or impaired absorption of, B12. In pernicious anemia the malabsorption is caused by the lack of the "intrinsic factor" in the stomach lining which makes it possible for the B12 to be properly absorbed in the intestines.

The most common intestinal cause of malabsorption is gluten intolerance.

The destructive reaction between the glutens and the intestinal lining hampers absorption of the foods, even those that have been digested. Surely the reader can now appreciate why we've repeatedly stressed the use of B12 injections to bypass the failing intestinal absorption mechanism.

Injected B12 is harmless, inexpensive and helpful. Celiacs are not the only ones benefited by its use. Even aged persons whose intestinal tissues function below par suffer from various degrees of malabsorption of ingested food elements. For such people, 1000 microgram injections at two- to four-week intervals are helpful. The aged have many neurological deficits. B12 injections are a simple modality to help support the function of their nerve cells and thus enhance their quality of life experience.

We all need to "Think celiac" and to this we should add "Think B12" so that our consciousness will be sensitive to these topics and we won't overlook these important physical handicaps.

10

DANGERS IN TOO MUCH GLUTEN

Are there dangers in the too liberal use of gluten? We believe that there can be. For example: We have recently had called to our attention (since the first printing of this volume) a medical research report wherein a group of healthy volunteers were fed 100 grams of gluten daily for a period of ten weeks. The investigators reported that at the end of the experimental period the subjects had begun to develop symptoms of celiac sprue.

We have also recently observed a case wherein a young adult man who had no known intestinal symptoms decided to become a vegetarian. To take the place of his former flesh food diet he ate heartily of "textured" vegetable protein meat analogs (substitutes) such as the canned gluten-based foods.

After a few months he developed classical symptoms of celiac disease and these symptoms were reversed when he adopted a totally gluten-free diet program while still adhering to a non-flesh diet.

In this case the man evidently had the genetic tendency toward gluten intolerance and only required an overabundance of the alpha-gliadin to trigger the manifestation of his gluten intolerance.

By way of contrast we can hardly assume that an entire series of apparently healthy young men who were fed 100 grams of pure gluten daily would all have a genetic predisposition to celiac disease. This raises the question of whether or not pure gluten, without the other naturally occurring substances in the gluten grains, might have some harmful effects on the intestines. We don't have an answer to this question but we do know that our benevolent Creator placed in natural food substances the proper components that are beneficial and complementary to each other.

As an example, we know that we can do much harm to individuals if we place them on a diet wherein the naturally occurring vitamins and minerals of whole wheat have been removed in the milling process.

In any event, this writer has no hesitancy in stating his convictions, based upon his clinical experiences and observations, that the so-called "health foods" based upon the devitalized and extracted gluten are *not* at all true health foods, and if used at all by those who might prefer them for whatever reason, they should be used exceedingly sparingly. Personally I am convinced that they should be excluded from so-called healthful diets.

Why not eat gluten in its naturally occurring form in the whole grains? Except in the case of gluten-intolerant persons, whole grains are true health foods, provided they have not been mauled and extracted by man and had their vital components removed or altered.

We ask again: Are there dangers in the liberal use of extracted gluten? I believe the answer is yes, there can be!

Protein-losing Enteropathy

The June 17, 1989 issue of *Lancet* carries an article that describes how much body protein loss could take place in debilitated aged individuals (in particular) who suffered from an intestinal infection due to *Clostridium difficile*. While Candida yeast is an altogether different microbe than the one noted above, without question the *Lancet* report illustrates how the diarrhea of gluten enteropathy and Candida enteropathy can also result in depletion of proteins from the body. Diligence in correcting any and all of these conditions is imperative.

Yeast and Streptomycin

I was recently asked to consult with a patient who gave the history of many years of intestinal yeast infection which seemed to have commenced after he received extended treatment with Streptomycin while in military service. It was thought that the drug had caused the moniliasis.

However, we found that he had clear symptomatic evidence of gluten intolerance. Whatever the role of the antibiotic, the gluten problem was also a factor, a factor often overlooked.

11

WHERE TO BEGIN

THE GLUTEN-FREE DIET

Gluten is a water-soluble, complex protein fragment present in some cereal grains, especially wheat and rye, and to a lesser extent in oats and barley. Gluten, usually considered a valuable nutrient, helps boost the volume of bread and other baked goods and gives them a good, non-crumbly texture.

The basis of a gluten-free diet is to avoid gluten *entirely:* that is, avoid grains, meals and flours made with wheat, oats, barley and rye. This must be done for the rest of your life! Today however, avoiding these grains and gluten is not as simple as it sounds.

Hidden Sources of Gluten

Decades ago, chemically altered starch (also known as food starch or modified food starch) was added to processed foods. Today it's in virtually *every* processed food product. This starch contains gluten because it's made from wheat. Besides starches, emulsifiers and stabilizers are also traditionally derived from wheat—the prime offender in terms of gluten content.

The glut of gluten-boosted foods continues, with wheat gluten now appearing as a binder, filler, bulking agent and even in medicine or vitamin tablets. Gluten is also often a constituent of meat and poultry products, sausages, textured protein meat extenders and meat substitutes. Canned meats may also contain a small portion of gluten.

Other hidden sources of gluten include, but are not limited to: imitation cheese, foods on steam tables at restaurants (where it's included to prevent foods from turning mushy), in MSG, in wheat germ (because of the way the germ is processed), malt (most breakfast cereals contain malt or malt extract, which can contain gluten), some alcoholic beverages, and pharmaceutical products (as an excipient).

As if all this isn't depressing or discouraging enough, there's more. Wheat flour may be lurking as a hidden ingredient in some ice creams, catsups, mayonnaise, self-rising corn meals and even in your instant coffee! (*Gluten Intolerance* by Beatrice Trum Hunter, Keats Publishing Inc., New Canaan, Conn., 1987.)

But wheat's not the only culprit. Even items labeled "wheat-free" can still contain gluten, so don't be taken in by that label. Also, since celiacs cannot tolerate even a tiny bit of gluten, products advertised as "low-gluten" or "for modified gluten diets" should be shunned like the plague they are to sufferers of celiac sprue.

The good news is, there *are* alternatives. Flours made from brown rice, potatoes, millet, corn, amaranth and quinoa can usually be tolerated.

The general and safest rule is, avoid *all* factory processed foods to avoid the possibility of ingesting gluten in a disguised form. Here in the Appendix we list a number of helpful books with recipes for those who are gluten intolerant. And further on we've included a few simple recipes for crackers and cereals, as well as dairy-free "milks" that you can use in the meantime.

Although living without gluten can seem like a hardship (especially for children), the alternative—a lifetime of feeling ill and ruining your digestive system—is much worse, is it not?

THE EATING TEST

Your investigation starts before you actually eliminate gluten from your diet, with a carefully kept diary in which you write down every morsel of food that you eat *several days before* you commence the gluten-free diet, along with any symptoms you feel.

Then, on the day you begin the gluten-free program and every day thereafter, continue to record all the food you've eaten, as well as how you're feeling that day. Some sufferers of celiac sprue can see within a day or two a real difference in how they feel, while others may need a week or even two or three to feel better.

To do the test as accurately as possible, you should also abstain from milk and milk products during this time, to eliminate the possibility that what's bothering you is milk (lactose) intolerance. You can use the lactose-free products suggested in this book. Also, stay away from soy products until the eating test is over.

After several weeks, you should see whether you have true gluten intolerance or not. At this time, if all signs point to this condition, you should continue to refrain from all gluten products.

A final note: If you experience typical celiac disease symptoms and a few weeks trial on the gluten-free diet has given you little or no relief, search harder for hidden sources of gluten in your foods. You must remove *every speck* of gluten or risk continuing misery.

Even if you don't have all the symptoms of CS, but you suspect you may have it, or perhaps you see signs of it in your children, try eating gluten-free for a few weeks. It can't hurt, and if it doesn't help you can always go back to eating wheat.

RECIPES FOR CELIACS

The next two chapters contain close to 100 recipes for gluten-free dishes of all kinds, and may be consulted as a kind of cookbook for the gluten-free way of eating. Here I would like to present a few basic recipes for celiacs as a brief demonstration that even such gluten-associated items such as breads and cereals can be prepared without gluten grains.

Breads and Crackers

My sister-in-law, Wanda Woodruff, has a gluten-intolerant husband, and has used her years of experience as a high-school home economics teacher to devise some extremely tasty gluten-free recipes, and in this one takes on the challenge of making a raised bread without gluten grains.

Wanda's Brown and White Rice Bread

Dissolve in a small bowl

2 Tbsp. sugar	1 Tbsp. xanthan gum
1¾ cups warm water	¼ tsp. salt
1 Tbsp. dry yeast	1 cup brown rice flour
¼ cup oil	1½ cup white rice flour
¼ cup sugar	2 eggs

Beat eggs well, then beat all ingredients together. Let rise, beat again, put in bread pan, let rise again. Bake at 350–375°F for 10 minutes, then cover with aluminum foil and bake for a further 50 minutes.

As I said, the absence of gluten makes the preparation of raised breads difficult, though not, as you see, impossible, but crackers of various kinds are quite easy to make, as are corn-based crepes, another of Wanda's specialties.

Without gluten grains it's rather difficult in the home to bake raised bread in the ordinary sense of the term. But crackers of various kinds are quite easy to make.

Corn-Carrot Crackers

The pulp left over from the extracting of juice from carrots is usually discarded, but this wastes good nutrients and excellent food fiber. We've found a valuable use for it in the making of crackers which can be used as "bread" at the table. (If desired, the carrot juice can be used too.)

6 cups corn flour	2 Tbsp. vanilla extract
3 or 4 bananas, ripe, mashed	5 cups grated carrot pulp
1 cup oil	2 cups apple sauce
6 cups boiling water	2 cups rice flour
1 cup finely ground coconut	3 Tbsp. brown sugar
	1 tsp. salt

As desired, additions can be made of quinoa flour, pea flour, tapioca flour, potato meal flour, etc.

Mix the various flours and the carrot pulp and then add the boiling water and continue mixing. Gradually add the other ingredients, adding vanilla last. More water may be needed as the batter should be fairly thin.

On six spots on a greased cookie sheet, ladle out about a tablespoonful or two of the batter and then slap the flat metal sheet firmly a few times onto the baking deck, causing the batter to spread out thinly and evenly. You can regulate the thickness by the thinness of the batter and by the number of slapping blows made with the metal sheet.

Bake in oven at 400°F. When the crackers begin to brown slightly around edges, remove them and allow to cool on cooling racks. When cooled they're ready to eat, or to place in bags and freeze for future use.

Corn-Rice Sticks

2 cups corn flour
¼ cup oil
2 cups ground nuts
  (optional)
2 cups cold water
2 cups brown rice flour

2 Tbsp. brown sugar (or
  molasses)
2 tsp. vanilla extract
1 tsp. ground cardamom
  seasoning

Fine sprinkling of sugar before placing rolled out dough in oven
(optional).

Combine all ingredients using only enough water to make a
stiff dough. Knead thoroughly. Roll out to thickness of pie crust
and cut in strips one inch by two inches long, or one can roll
out dough on cookie sheet and mark. Bake at 350°F. until light
golden brown. Do not let them get too dark or they will be
bitter. Yield seven or eight dozen. These may be frozen in a
deep freeze in plastic bags. They're nice for school lunches,
picnics, or served with soup.

Wanda's Crepes

Blend well in blender
2½ cups water
1½ cups rice flour (or half
  and half rice and corn
  flour)

½ tsp. salt

After the mixture is well blended, let it sit for 5 minutes so
that the moisture goes into the flour. Pour in crepe-sized portions into a hot nonstick skillet, cook until dry on top and
brown on bottom; turn and brown other side.

If the crepes tend to stick, they may not be sufficiently
baked. They may be stored in the freezer in bags with wax
paper between crepes.

Breakfast Cereals

For breakfast cereals celiacs have the choice of a number of dry cereals that are gluten-free and are available in many markets. Cooked cereals offer certain problems. There is of course Cream of Rice (white rice) and corn meal. One source of cracked or ground brown rice was said to be very delicious, but when I checked with the large mill that cracks it and asked what kind of mill they used to process the brown rice they admitted to me that they used the same mill as that used to grind wheat. But they claimed they "cleaned" the mill between each use. Celiacs know that such brief "cleaning" may not be enough. Traces of wheat flour may remain and lodge in the ground rice. But we've located a couple of safe products as follows:

Quick Brown Rice—Arrowhead Mills, Hereford, Texas. These rice kernels have been preheated so that they are partially processed and they offer a very tasty and nutritious breakfast delight that cooks in but a few minutes. If the 12 oz. packages are not available in your local stores you can phone the Arrowhead Mills and purchase the packages in case lots.

Quinoa—pronounced keen-wah, these are tiny seeds about the size of sesame seeds that originated in South America. The seeds are now grown in the U.S. They are highly nutritious and their protein and amino acids analysis compares favorably with soy and wheat, in fact exceeding these two foods in some categories. Quinoa is highly digestible and delicious and cooks easily.

As far as I know the seeds have not as yet been analyzed for alpha-gliadin content but I have tried it with about ten celiacs and none have reported any adverse intestinal effects. The seeds are not members of the grass family such as wheat but botanically are of the *Chenopodium* family and related to the common garden weed, lamb's quarters. Theoretically they should not contain the adverse gliadin.

The cereal grains may be purchased in health food shops.

Quinoa is also available as flour to use in baking and they now have an elbow macaroni pasta product which is delicious. We have used these products without any untoward effects.

Milk-Free Recipes

Individuals suffering from lactose intolerance may wish to completely eliminate all market milk and milk products from the diet; this would be especially appropriate for persons who might also be allergic to the proteins of milk. In the latter persons no amount of treatment of dairy milk would bring relief from the allergy to the milk proteins.

Accordingly, we will list a number of milk and cream substitutes made wholly from foods of the vegetable kingdom. The majority of these are copied from our 1963 cookbook *Rx Recipes* by Rosenvold and Rosenvold.

When the recipe states "liquefy" it naturally means to liquefy the materials in an electric blender. Several of the recipes call for the use of cashew nuts. Warning: Cashew nuts are grown and shelled in the tropics. In the shelling-out process they are often handled without regard to proper sanitation standards. Therefore cashew nuts should *never* be used raw. They need to be washed and then lightly toasted in order to "sterilize" them from contamination.

Cashews: Place a quantity of whole or halved cashew nuts in a colander in the sink. Pour several quarts of boiling water over them. After draining, place on cookie sheets in one layer only and place in oven preheated to 375° F. for 10 to 15 minutes. Watch the nuts carefully and when they just begin to turn a golden brown along the edges, remove from oven and allow to cool in a large open pan for several hours until thoroughly dry and hard. They are then ready to eat, or use in cooking, or to store in refrigerator or freezer.

Milk and Cream Substitutes: Almond, pecan and cashew milks may be made in much the same way, using dates or just the honey. If you like milk thicker, use less water. For thinner milk, use more water. For desserts, use more honey.

Cashew milk is better if the cashews are first toasted in the oven at 375° until light golden brown.

If walnuts make your mouth sore, try using the Franquette variety. We have found that even people with allergy to walnuts can tolerate this variety.

Pecan Milk

1 cup shelled pecans   ⅛ tsp. salt
1 qt. cold water

Liquefy, add water and salt.

If liquefier is not available put pecans through the finest blade of a meat grinder, then add water and salt. Place in sauce pan and heat until almost boiling, stirring constantly. Remove from sauce pan. Cool and refrigerate.

Unsweetened Walnut Milk

1 qt. water   ¼ tsp. salt
1 cup shelled walnuts

Liquefy.

Almond Cream

1 cup blanched almonds   ⅛ tsp. salt
2 cups cold water

Liquefy. If heavy cream is desired reduce water as desired. A few drops of vanilla may be added.

Coconut Milk #1

1 cup water   ½ cup grated fresh coconut
1 tsp. honey   ¼ tsp. salt

Liquefy and serve.

Coconut Milk #2

Remove coconut from shell. Peel off brown skin. Cut into small pieces. Put into liquefier with all of coconut milk and add enough water to liquefy easily. Squeeze through cloth. Add 1 Tbsp. honey or sugar. If less liquid is used this will be thick and makes very good topping in place of cream. Use it sparingly—it is very rich.

Cashew Cream

Cover blades of liquefier with water. Feed cashew nuts into water slowly until thick as cream. Add two Tbsp. honey and a little salt. This makes a nice topping for desserts.

Walnut Milk

1 qt. water   1 cup dates pitted
½ cup honey   (optional)
1 cup walnut meats

Liquefy, using blender or vitamizer.

Almond Milk

¾ cup almonds, blanched   ¼ tsp. salt
3¼ cups water   1 tsp. vanilla
½ Tbsp. honey

Blend almonds with small amount of water first; then add remaining water and ingredients. Whiz until smooth. Strain, chill and serve.

Sesame Milk

1 cup sesame seeds, light	2 cups water
¼ tsp. salt	⅛ cup honey

Bring sesame seeds and water to a boil, simmer 10 minutes. Add remaining ingredients. Blend until smooth. Chill and serve.

Cashew Milk

Blend:

1 cup cashew meal	1 cup hot water

Add:

¼ tsp. salt	1 Tbsp. honey
1 tsp. vanilla	3 cups water

Blend until smooth. Chill and serve.

Rice Milk

⅔ cup hot, cooked rice	1 tsp. salt
⅓ cup cashew meal	1 Tbsp. honey
1 tsp. vanilla	3 cups hot water

Blend until smooth: Chill and serve.

Obviously many modifications of the above collection of recipes can be made to suit taste and materials on hand. Nuts are highly nutritious, but many of them have a rather high fat content and should be used very sparingly. This is especially true with celiacs who have difficulty with fat assimilation as a part of their intestinal problem.

Banana Ice Cream

Peel and freeze several ripe bananas. When thoroughly frozen, run them through a juicer, adding whatever fruit is desired (fresh or frozen or canned strawberries, peaches, blueberries etc.). Even strawberry jam is fine. Don't forget pineapple and other tropical fruits. Fluid vanilla extract may be added if desired. If not mixed thoroughly in the machine, stir. Ground nuts may be added in the stirring. Add sweetening if needed.

This dessert is ready to serve and eat immediately, or it may be placed in a covered vessel and stored in the freezer for later.

If the creamed mixture is run through an ice-cream mixer machine and frozen gently and slowly, it will have a smoother texture than if the creamed mixture is placed in the freezer and allowed to super-cool by itself.

There is hardly any limit to the flavors and textures you can dream up with this lactose-free ice cream recipe.

Hot Spices

At this juncture I wish to bring up the complicating role of hot dietary condiments in aggravating gastrointestinal disease and thus complicating both diagnosis and treatment. I well recall a physician from Mexico many years ago citing the free use of hot peppers etc. in the causation of gastro-intestinal diseases in her nation. She was much concerned over these practices of her people.

More recently, a close friend, in middle adult life, who loved spicy hot food and thought he tolerated it well, found that he had lower colonic symptoms of burning and distress. Investigation revealed a cancerous polyp which required radical surgical removal. Now, after his surgery he is determined to give up all hot, spicy food and not further "insult" the delicate linings of his intestinal tract.

Why do I bring in a non-CS case by way of illustration? Simply to call attention to celiacs the fact that with their restricted diets they may crave something by way of spices to "liven up" their sometimes monotonous diets. But by indulging in the hot spices they may actually inflict further damage on their delicate intestinal linings which are already severely damaged by the alpha-gliadin from their earlier use of gluten foods.

Remember, your intestinal lining may not be visible to you, but it's just about as delicate as the mucous lining of the eyes or the nose.

I realize it may not be the most popular undertaking for me to suggest to patients that they forever foreswear the use of strong condiments for the good of their intestines. But would I be an honest physician if I failed to warn patients or readers that the strong condiments can harm their already damaged and very delicate tissues?

There are harmless and mild food seasonings that persons with perverted tastes can learn to use as substitute seasonings while they are re-educating their taste buds. I appeal to celiacs: Be gentle with such intestinal linings as you have left. Treat them right and they will treat you right.

12

GLUTEN-FREE RECIPES

This chapter represents dozens of recipes for a variety of dishes made without gluten, from breakfast foods to desserts. Most are from my wife's and my book *Rx Recipes: A Guide to Healthful Food Preparation*, published by Rosenvold Publications.

You will notice that some recipes call for gluten-free bread crumbs. If you don't wish to provide your own from one of the breads or crackers for which recipes are given here, these bread crumbs may be obtained in many health food stores or from producers listed in the Resources section. Please note that, wherever milk is mentioned, nut milk or rice milk or coconut milk can be substituted if you or someone you are cooking for is lactose-intolerant. Or you can use milk treated especially for those who can't break down lactose.

Instead of Bread

Corn Meal Mush

1 cup corn meal
2½ cups boiling water

¾ cups cold water
1 tsp. salt

Blend the corn meal with the cold water so that it is smooth and has no lumps. Add boiling water slowly, beating it quickly to avoid lumping. Add salt and stir as it boils. Set in a double boiler and cook for half an hour. Serve with grated apple or raisins.

Corn Pone

1½ cups corn meal
2 Tbsp. veg. oil
1 tsp. salt

1 cup grated carrots
3 Tbsp. brown sugar
1 cup boiling water

Mix all dry ingredients, pour over the mixture the hot water, stirring until blended. Oil iron muffin or iron corn mold. Bake for about one hour. Watch that they do not burn. Oven 425°.

Corn Bread

1 pkg. dry yeast
2¼ cups warm water
1 tsp. lecithin
3 Tbsp. veg. oil
3 Tbsp. brown sugar

1 cup corn meal (burr grind)
½ cup potato flour
½ cup rice flour
1 tsp. salt

Put yeast in warm water with lecithin. Beat well. Add sugar, oil and salt. Stir and beat in the flour and corn meal. Pour batter into a greased baking tin. Cover and let rise. When light and double its bulk, bake at 350° for 30 minutes.

Tomato-Lima Bean Soup

1 cup tomato paste or home-
  canned puree to make ½
  cup
2½ cups water
½ cup lima bean puree

½ cup milk
1 tsp. salt
1 Tbsp. oil
1 tsp. chopped chives
¼ tsp. celery salt

Put water, tomato, lima beans and milk in liquefier or run lima
beans through a sieve. Add salt, celery salt, oil and chives. If
too thick add a little more water. Heat but do not let boil.

Tomato Avocado Soup

1 qt. tomato juice
1 ripe avocado
¼ tsp. salt

1 tsp. chopped chives
½ cup water
½ cup milk

Heat tomato juice, add salt and chives. Liquefy avocado using
the water and milk. If one does not have a liquifier mash and
whip avocado with fork. Pour into heated tomato juice, stirring
briskly. Do not let boil.

Red Onion Soup

1 large sweet red onion
  chopped fine
1 qt. potato water into
  which 1 Tbsp. potato
  flour has been blended

2 tsp. freshly chopped
  parsley
salt to taste

Cook until onions are soft, add:

1 cup rich milk

1 Tbsp. vegetable oil

Reheat but do not let boil. Serve at once.

Health Soup

5 medium tomatoes
½ large ripe avocado
1 cup carrot juice

½ tsp. onion powder
Pinch garlic powder
1 cup celery juice

Put tomatoes and avocado in blender and liquefy, then add carrot and celery juice, onion and garlic powder. Pour into double boiler and heat until hot but do not boil. Add 2 tsp. freshly chopped parsley and serve at once.

Creamed Almond-Corn Soup

2 cups creamed style corn
1 cup water
1 medium sized onion chopped
1 small bay leaf
1 stalk celery

2 Tbsp. margarine or veg. oil
½ cup ground almonds or almond butter
1 tsp. salt
1 cup milk

Combine corn, water, onion, bay leaf and celery. Cook in double boiler 15 minutes. Do not boil. Strain through sieve. Put back in double boiler. Combine fat, almonds, salt and milk making a smooth paste. Combine all together and place in double boiler. Bring almost to a boil. Serve hot.

Hearty Main and Side Dishes

Jacob's Lentil Stew

1 cup lentils
4 cups cold water
1 cup tiny white onions
1 clove garlic
3 carrots, sliced

2 tsp. salt
½ tsp. cardamom seed
2 tsp. lemon juice
1 cup diced potato

Wash, then soak lentils overnight in 4 cups of cold water. In the morning cook lentils ½ hour and then add all other ingredients.

Okra and Rice

½ cup cooked brown rice
1 cup canned okra, or boiled
  fresh okra, diced
1½ cups tomatoes
¾ tsp. salt

¼ tsp. thyme
½ onion chopped fine
1 Tbsp. oil
1 tsp. flour

Cook onion in oil until brown. Mix together with all other ingredients, pour into oiled baking dish and bake for ¾ hour.

Baked Okra

Wash, stem and cook okra in about ½ cup water. When soft, drain and roll in this mixture:

⅓ cup corn meal
⅓ cup brewer's yeast flakes

½ tsp. salt
½ cup potato meal

Lay okra, rolled in above mixture in an oiled baking dish. Bake at 375° F. until golden brown, turning once or twice.

Baked Harvard Beets

3 cups peeled raw diced
  beets
⅓ cup sugar
2 Tbsp. veg. oil

⅓ cup lemon juice
½ tsp. salt
½ cup water
3 Tbsp. flour

Make a sauce of the oil, flour, sugar, lemon juice and water, using a low heat. Pour beets into a casserole; pour the sauce over the beets; place into a cold oven and bake for 1½ hours at 350°.

English Peas with Mushrooms

1 qt. shelled peas
½ cup water
Cook until almost done

1 cup sliced mushrooms
⅓ cup sliced green onions
2 Tbsp. oil

Put oil, mushrooms and onions into frying pan and cook until done. Turn into peas and bring to boil. (Water from peas should be gone.) Add salt to taste and serve.

Baked Kidney Beans

3 cups kidney beans
2 large onions sliced
2 cups canned tomatoes
3 Tbsp. chopped green pepper

1 Tbsp. salt
2 Tbsp. brown sugar
3 Tbsp. veg. oil

Soak beans overnight. Parboil with onions in morning and then turn into bean pot. Add rest of ingredients and bake slowly for 5 or 6 hours keeping enough water on beans to keep them from sticking to the bottom. Beans should not be dry when done. Good served with beet tops and gluten-free bread.

Swedish Brown Beans

2 cups kidney beans. Soak overnight in cold water. In the morning put them on the stove and stew them. Cook them gently until they begin to get tender then add:

2 tsp. salt
⅓ cup brown sugar

¼ cup lemon juice

Pour into bean pot and bake slowly at about 325° for about two or three hours. Do not cook dry, add water when necessary but have beans nicely brown when done.

Peanut Butter Loaf

2 cups grated raw carrots
1 cup cooked rice
½ cup shelled peanuts.
   Liquefy or chop fine.
½ cup gluten-free bread
   crumbs

3 Tbsp. chopped onion
1 cup milk
3 Tbsp. oil
⅛ tsp. sage
¼ tsp. salt

Mix all together. Cover and let stand about ½ hour. Pour into greased baking dish. Cover and bake at 350° for 1 hour.

Baked Peanuts

1 pound shelled and skinned peanuts. Soak overnight in cold water that covers peanuts one inch. In the morning add:

1 tsp. salt
¼ cup molasses

1 tsp. sugar
1 small onion

Pour into a bean pot and bake slowly until soft.

Walnut Roast

1½ cups rich milk
1½ cups gluten-free bread
   crumbs
1 cup ground walnuts
1 tsp. salt
1 medium onion chopped
   fine

2 Tbsp. vegetable oil
2 Tbsp. parsley chopped
   fine
1 tsp. salt

Sauté the onions in the oil. Mix all ingredients together. Let stand ½ hour covered. Turn into an oiled baking dish. Bake for 1 hour at 350°.

Pecans may be used instead of walnuts.

Cooked Lentils

Clean and wash 2 cups lentils and soak overnight in cold water. Water should be about two inches above lentils. In the morning cook in covered kettle in same water, adding 1½ tsp. salt and 2 Tbsp. oil. Cook slowly for 1 hour.

Lentil Patties

Using small blade on meat grinder, grind 1 cup walnut meats and 3 stalks of celery.

Sauté one medium-sized chopped onion, turn into mixing bowl and add above ingredients. To this add:

3 cups finely ground gluten-free bread crumbs
2 Tbsp. chopped parsley, or
1 Tbsp. dried parsley
1 tsp. salt

1½ cups mashed cooked lentils
1 cup water or more to make right moisture to mold into patties

Let stand in covered bowl for ½ hour. Form into patties. Place on oiled cookie sheet and bake, or brown in oiled frying pan using medium flame.

Lentil Patties II

2 cups cooked mashed lentils
3 Tbsp. green onion
3 cups mashed potato

2 Tbsp. vegetable oil
½ tsp. chopped parsley
salt to taste

Soften onion in oil over a low heat. Put mashed lentils, parsley, salt and potatoes in bowl. Add onions and oil. Stir mixture. Form into patties and brown lightly on oiled skillet.

Baked Lentils

Pour 2 cups cooked lentils into baking dish and add:

1 cup stewed tomatoes
½ cup chopped sweet green
  peppers
2 Tbsp. oil if not added
  when cooking lentils

½ tsp. salt if not added when
  cooking lentils
½ cup chopped green onions

Bake slowly at 325° for ¾ hour.

Sunflower Loaf

1 cup ground walnuts
½ cup gluten-free bread
  crumbs
½ cup grated raw potato
1 tsp. salt

1 cup milk
3 Tbsp. grated onion
½ cup ground sunflower
  seeds
1 Tbsp. oil

Mix well. Let stand with cover on for ½ hour. Bake for 1 hour
at 350° F.

Baked Split Peas

3 cups split peas that have
  been cooked
2 cups cooked brown rice
2 cups canned tomatoes
½ cup onion, chopped fine

1 tsp. veg. oil
¾ cup gluten-free bread
  crumbs
1 tsp. salt

Oil baking dish and make layers of the peas, rice, tomatoes and
onion. Sprinkle with salt. Cover with oiled gluten-free bread
crumbs and bake at 400° for 20 minutes. Serve with white sauce
or brown gravy.

Peanut Roast

2 cups grated raw carrots
½ cup peanut butter
1 cup milk
3 Tbsp. oil
1 cup cooked rice

2 Tbsp. grated onion
½ cup gluten-free bread
  crumbs
½ tsp. salt

Cream milk and peanut butter. Add oil, then other ingredients. Turn into oiled baking dish. Bake slowly at 375° one hour. Serve with tomato sauce.

Savory Garbanzos

2 Tbsp. vegetable oil
¼ cup green pepper slivers
3 cups cooked garbanzos
  (chickpeas)

½ cup small onion rings
1½ cups stewed tomatoes

Wash garbanzos. Add twice as much cold water as the beans and soak overnight. Cook in same water in pressure cooker for 1¼ hours. If pressure cooker is not available use heavy covered kettle and cook for 6 hours. Simmer onion rings and peppers in oil for 3 minutes. Add stewed tomatoes. Let simmer only a few minutes to blend flavors, then add to garbanzos. Stir and serve.

Sauces and Dressings

Avocado Mayonnaise

Beat ripe avocado in liquefier or electric beater adding about ⅓ cup pineapple juice, a pinch of salt and a few drops of lemon juice.

Basic White Sauce

	Oil or margarine	Rice flour	Salt	Milk
Thin	1 Tbsp.	1 Tbsp.	½ tsp.	1 cup
Medium	2 Tbsp.	2 Tbsp.	½ tsp.	1 cup
Thick	4 Tbsp.	4 Tbsp.	½ tsp.	1 cup

Blend all ingredients together until smooth. Cook in double boiler.

White Sauce Variations

3 Tbsp. lemon juice with 1 tsp. grated lemon rind
3 Tbsp. orange juice with 1 tsp. grated orange rind
2 Tbsp. lime juice with 2 tsp. grated lime rind and 2 Tbsp. sugar
3 Tbsp. minced parsley
2 Tbsp. minced pimientos

Lemon Sauce

½ cup sugar
1 tsp. corn or potato starch
1 cup water
1½ Tbsp. lemon juice

½ tsp. grated lemon rind
⅛ tsp. salt
2 Tbsp. oil

Liquefy all ingredients and pour into saucepan. Cook at low heat until clear and thick. Without liquefier combine sugar, starch and water. Pour into saucepan and cook at low heat stirring constantly. Add lemon juice, lemon rind, oil and salt. Cook until clear and thick.

Mint Sauce

2 Tbsp. chopped fresh mint
2 Tbsp. sugar

2 Tbsp. lemon juice
2 Tbsp. water

Pour boiling water over the mint, add lemon juice and sugar, and let stand in a warm place until sugar is dissolved.

Cashew Salad Dressing

⅔ cup lightly toasted cashew
   nuts
2 Tbsp. chopped fresh
   parsley (optional)
1 Tbsp. chopped chives
   (optional)

2 Tbsp. lemon juice
¼ cup corn oil
⅓ cup water
Sprinkle of salt or celery salt

Place nuts, oil, water, salt, parsley and chives in blender (preferably the kind that uses an inverted ½ pint glass fruit jar) and run the blades until the ingredients are finely chopped and emulsified. Then with a spoon or fork gently stir in the lemon juice to taste. Ready to serve. Store in refrigerator. If by the following day the dressing has thickened it may be thinned by stirring in a little oil or water.

Salad Dressing

½ cup sunflower seeds
½ cup cooked brown rice
¼ to ⅓ cup lemon juice (or
   less to taste)
½ tsp. onion salt

¼ tsp. garlic powder—or 1
   or 2 cloves
½ tsp. salt (optional)
¼ tsp. dill weed (optional)

Put all in blender with 1 cup of hot water. Blend until smooth.

This salad dressing may be used as any type of dressing or mayonnaise would be used. May be used for potato salads and also for dips such as dipping artichoke leaves, etc.

Golden Sauce

Blend cooked potatoes and cooked carrots with lemon juice and other spices or herbs as desired. Add water to thin. Whiz until smooth.

Golden Salad

2 cups apricot juice	6 pecan halves
2 cups tangerine juice	4 Tbsp. agar-agar
2 tsp. sugar	
1 cup Thompson seedless grapes	

Boil the juices and sugar with the agar-agar. When clear and no agar-agar is present set aside for about five minutes, then add grapes. Place a pecan half in the bottom of each mold and pour in the agar-agar. This makes a beautiful salad.

Yellow and White Salad

4 cups grated carrots	1 head lettuce
⅔ cup grated white turnip	salad dressing (see recipe,
½ tsp. salt	previous page)
½ cup diced celery	

Mix carrot, turnip, salt and celery. Add ⅓ cup salad dressing and stir. Chill. Arrange lettuce in a nest and with ice cream scoop place one scoop of salad mixture in center of lettuce. A strip of red pimiento adds a festive touch.

Desserts

Apricot Candy

Steam ¾ cup dried apricots about 5 minutes in ½ cup water. Cool and put through food chopper.

Add:

⅓ cup coconut grated, fresh or dried	1 tsp. lemon juice
¾ cup chopped pecans	1 tsp. lemon rind
	1 tsp. orange juice

Mix thoroughly. Form into balls. Roll into coconut or confectioners sugar. Place in refrigerator for several hours. These are nice for picnics, for travel or for school lunches.

Chinese Almond Cookies

2 cups brown rice flour	¼ cup vegetable oil
1 cup powdered sugar	7 Tbsp. milk
½ tsp. salt	1 tsp. vanilla
¾ cup blanched almonds	1 tsp. almond extract

Sift flour, sugar and salt. Put the almonds into a liquefier. This will chop them very fine. Pour into mixing bowl. Pour oil into measuring cup and add milk, vanilla and almond extract. Stir into the dry ingredients, knead with hands to form a ball. Roll out on bread board to ¼ inch thickness, cut with cookie cutter, place on cookie sheet and bake for 10 or 12 minutes at 350°.

Health Candy

½ cup ground dried apricots	½ cup ground pecan meats
½ cup ground dried pears	½ cup raisins, ground
½ cup dried dates	2 Tbsp. lemon juice

Mix all together. Form into a roll and wrap in wax paper. Refrigerate overnight. Slice in ¼ inch slices with sharp knife.

13

SPROUTING SEEDS

Sprouted seeds are an excellent source of nutrition, and can extend the gluten-free repertoire considerably—as long, of course, as sprouted wheat, rye, barley or oats are not used. After a discussion of the nutritional value of sprouts and how to sprout seeds, there is an extensive recipe section, drawn from Martha Oliver's *Add a Few Sprouts* (Keats Publishing), which will allow you to explore the interesting and healthful culinary possibilities of these miniature vegetables.

Note that some dishes call for soy sauce. Examine the label of any soy sauce you consider buying to make sure that wheat is not an ingredient.

Seeds are among the richest, most nutritious of foods that are available. A seed contains the elements needed to reproduce the next generation of the plant. Seeds, therefore, are rich sources of proteins, some carbohydrate, and a number of minerals and vitamins. Some of the better edible vegetable seeds are sunflower seeds, sesame seed, pumpkin and squash seeds. Seeds of the ordinary Hubbard squash are readily dried and the interior kernel is highly nutritious.

One of the finest delicacies among seeds are hulled sunflower seeds. The Russians use them freely and also use the pressed oil of the seed.

I can recommend hulled sunflower seeds to be eaten whole or ground up in cereals, breads or roasts. A cupful supplies half of the daily requirement of thiamin and five times the daily vitamin E requirement as well as other vitamins. The 25 percent protein is of the finest type. Its oil is one of the highest in unsaturated fatty acid content.

Seed Sprouts

In order to enhance the value of seeds and at the same time make available a tasty food, man has learned to sprout seeds. Most people are acquainted with Chinese bean sprouts, which are made from fresh, clean soy beans or a type of bean called the Mung bean. All that is necessary is that the seed be soaked for an appropriate length of time, after which the seeds are placed in a receptacle that permits a warm and moist atmosphere. In a few hours, depending upon the size of the seed, the seeds will sprout and in 3 to 5 days the young plants are ready to "harvest."

The sprouting of seeds for human consumption can be accomplished in many ways. Seeds can be wrapped in moist towels after the initial soaking period, or they can be placed in glasses, or tubs, or receptacles, being properly moistened and rinsed several times daily. However, these methods are a bit time-consuming. A better method is to place the seeds in some sort of vessel of proper porosity which is in turn set in a shallow vessel of water. For this purpose a baked clay dish that has not been glazed is very suitable. These can be obtained from pottery factories or health food stores and are usually called "bisque" vessels. These, if set into a shallow vessel of water will absorb a small amount of water, but will not fill up with water. After placing a single layer of seeds in these vessels, the vessel is covered to exclude light and also to keep the atmosphere moist within the vessel. In 3 to 5 days vitamin-rich sprouts are produced.

It has been shown that legume sprouts of various types will produce so much abscorbic acid that one average salad serving supplies about half the daily adult requirement of vitamin C. Thus even in arctic or semi-arctic areas it is possible during the wintertime to grow fresh vitamins indoors, and it is not necessary to depend upon citrus fruits and other imported fruits to supply a substantial daily portion of vitamin C. Some of these experiments have even shown an increase in the B vitamins in the case of Mung beans as compared to the amount of B complex found in the dry seeds. Even vitamin A is produced in moderate quantity after the tops of the sprouts have begun to turn green.

Some of the easiest seeds to sprout are alfalfa, red clover, radish, lentils, peas, and mung beans. Seeds for sprouting must be cleaned carefully so that no broken seeds are soaked and placed in the sprouting apparatus for they will not sprout; they will only ferment. Needless to say, seeds to be used for sprouting should not have been treated by chemicals and insecticides which are often used on seeds that are prepared for soil planting. In securing seeds, we would advise the consumer to check this factor very carefully.

The Method

Place an appropriate amount of the clean seeds in a cup of warm water and after washing them to remove any dust and obvious dirt allow them to soak for the appropriate period of time as noted in the table herewith. It may be desirable if there is considerable color or stain on the seeds to rinse them several times during the soaking period. After the soaking period the seeds are poured out into the sprouting receptacle, whether this be. a bisque ceramic dish, or a paper-maché dish, or whether it be a cloth, or other apparatus, they are plated out into a thin layer, covered, and placed in a warm dark place. The back of the kitchen gas range is a suitable place because there is some warmth and yet it is not too hot to prevent germination. The sprouting seeds should be checked at least once or twice daily and water added to the water receptacle, changing the water as needed. In some instances, such as in the case of beans, it is advisable to wash the seeds themselves once or twice daily. As the seeds begin to sprout, if any obviously broken seeds are noted they should be picked out and discarded.

Seeds	Soaking time	Correct amount for one seeding	Ready to use
Radish	4 hours	2 teaspoons	3-5 days
Alfalfa	8 hours	1 teaspoon	3-5 days
Red clover	8 hours	1 teaspoon	3-5 days
Grains	8 hours	2 tablespoons	3-4 days
Mung beans	8 hours	¼ cup	3-6 days
Lentils	8 hours	¼ cup	3-6 days

On or about the third day many of these sprouts will be ready. However, some prefer to leave them for five days in order to obtain larger sprouts which will contain larger quantities of vitamins and be more nutritious. In the case of bean sprouts it is advisable at that time to wash them in cool water before use or serving. It is of interest to note that the vitamin C production is decreased if the sprouts are allowed to be exposed to light too long. Therefore, they should not be exposed during their sprouting period and they should be served as fresh as possible. It is also important that the sprouts not be allowed to become dry as some of them will turn brown if dried between the time of removal from the sprouting apparatus and the time of serving.

Some sprouts develop their maximum vitamin C content in about four or five days, others take as long as ten days. It is not necessary to be so accurate as to wait to the very last day, for some sprouts become too old and are not so palatable when they become old. Therefore, it is better to eat them at three to six days of age. Cooking tends to destroy any vitamin C found in sprouts. Therefore it is important that sprouts generally be eaten raw, or cooked very lightly as in the case of mung beans which are used in Chinese dishes. In the table above we have given the suggested quantities of seeds to be used for an average small family to produce one serving of sprouts. This can be made in various multiples, depending upon how many sprouts are needed.

The Use of Seed Sprouts

No doubt many individuals have not tasted raw seed sprouts and at first they may taste strange. However, with a little bit of practice in preparing and serving them and with the realization that they furnish good nutrients the average consumer can learn to relish seed sprouts. We would suggest that you start with alfalfa seeds which are very palatable. Alfalfa may be eaten plain, or sprinkled over salads, or used in soups. Red clover sprouts are much like those of alfalfa except that their taste is somewhat stronger. Their use is similar. Lentils have an unusual taste and are very suitable for use in mixed salads. Radishes are very delicious and are very easy to sprout. Their taste is very mild. They are very acceptable in salads. In experiments we conducted some years ago radish seeds produced a very large quantity of vitamin C as compared to other seeds.

IN CONCLUSION

We receive much correspondence (and many phone calls) from persons needing help with gluten problems. So many of them reveal a similar pattern. In babyhood perhaps much crying and vomiting and diarrhea, which eases up in a few months or years. Then a period of some years of relative quiescence after which intestinal symptoms return and after getting shunted around from physician to physician, finally someone stumbles on the diagnosis of celiac disease. Maybe some readers of these very lines have friends or relatives going through just this kind of experience right now. There is a woeful lack of information out there concerning gluten and all that pertains thereto.

I wish to express deep appreciation to readers who take the time to tell us of interesting cases or personal experiences. It's only as we all share these bits of information that we can all gain a clearer picture of the problems created in many lives by that fine protein food, gluten, which some persons through genetic defects cannot seem to be able to tolerate. Thank you one and all.

APPENDIX A

CELIAC UPDATE, JUNE 1991

Whereas a few years ago there was a comparatively limited number of research reports in the medical journals dealing with Celiac Disease (CD), now there seems to be a veritable stream of medical journal reports issuing from research centers dealing with various phases of CD.

Some of these set forth new views on the nature of CD, but others serve to reinforce some of the concepts which we have set forth in earlier essays in this book. In appendix A we will comment on these new findings and set forth for readers how some of the fundamentals which we delineated in earlier pages are being buttressed more and more as time passes.

Infertility

Millions of couples sorrow over their infertility—inability to bear children. Millions of dollars are spent each year for sophisticated tests and procedures to overcome or circumvent this disability. Individual couples may sometimes spend thousands of dollars in the process—sometimes fruitlessly. Sometimes the fault may lie in the female and sometimes in the male partner.

A recent report from Ireland (*Ulster Med. Journal* 57[1]: 88-89, 1988) details a case of infertility of at least three years' duration. Merely two months after undertaking a gluten-free (GF) diet, the individual was able to conceive. The investigators mention that there have been other cases of infertility (both male and female) with fertility restored by changing to a GF diet.

We know of no extensive data on how dependable this method for overcoming infertility might be—statistically. And in no way would we wish to lead to the impression that this method is a cure-all. But a trial of a GF diet by both parties for several months might merit consideration, if it is seriously believed that there is other evidence that CD exists. Certainly the dietary trial costs essentially nothing but some diligent kitchen effort.

Amenorrhoea (lack of menstruation)

A 19-year-old girl who had proven CD had never menstruated. Yet a mere 22 days after starting a GF diet she menstruated for the first time in her life. During the follow-up for 2 years her menstruations remained normal.

Another young CD woman, age 21, had never menstruated. Various tests revealed definite malabsorbtion problems. Only 34 days after being placed on a GF diet she had her first menstrual period ever, and has had normal menses ever since that time. (*Digestion*, 8: 509-510, 1973.)

Articular Diseases (such as arthritis)

There is evidence of a strong relationship between vertebral arthritis and "inflammations of the gut (intestines) in man." (*Acta Clin. Belg.* 45 (1):24-24, 1990.

Adenoma of Villi in Small Intestines

The investigators reported a malignancy of the small intestines originating in the villi which are the site of damage in CD.

Small bowel malignancies are rare. It is known that CD tends to favor the development of intestinal malignancies. All the more reason for seriously treating CD with a GF diet in the hope of preventing malignancies. (*Am. J. of Gastroenterology* 85(6):748-751, June 1990.)

Late "Onset" Of Celiac Disease

CD, being a genetic disorder, it is usually true that a careful medical history will reveal that there were actually evidences of CD early in life. But now come findings from Ireland that a negative family history may not be assurance that CD cannot become apparent in late 40', or even in elderly years. Physicians should be alert to the possibility of CD affecting even elderly persons who present themselves with obscure medical problems. (*Irish Med. J.* 77(2):35-36, 1984.)

Epilepsy

Recent findings seem to indicate that a certain type of left temporal (brain) lobe epilepsy is much more prevalent in persons with CD. We await further information on this startling finding. We should not forget that we have earlier pointed out that in CD, neurotoxins are produced in the gut, which after absorbtion into the blood stream can travel to distant tissues and there produce localized disease. *Dermatitis Herpetiformis* is one such example.

Aphthous Stomatitis—("Canker" Sores in the Mouth)

We have known for many years that "canker" sores in the mouth were sometimes associated with vitamin B deficiency. So also with food allergies. For example, I have known a person who developed allergy to soy products and when he would eat them tiny painful ulcers would develop along the sides of his tongue. Often at the same time circumscribed painful areas would develop in his stomach. These we believed were similar tiny ulcers such as seen on the tongue. When the soy was discontinued the mouth ulcers would heal and when the pain there went away, so also did the pained areas in the stomach, probably indicating that the gastric ulcers also healed.

Now we learn from several medical journal reports that these mouth ulcers can also be associated with CD. One report (in *Gut* 21:223-226, 1980) found two cases of the mouth ulcers in 50 patients with CD.

In another report (in *Digestive Diseases & Sciences* 26[8]:737-740, 1981) out of 20 patients with recurrent aphthous ulcers, 25% showed favorable responses to a withdrawal of gluten from the diet. In this study none had demonstrable intestinal lesions. Either they did not have CD, or else the disease was in such early stages that the intestinal lesions could not be demonstrated on biopsy. (Compare with the report from Holland that follows.)

In a report from Holland (*Netherlands J. of Med.* 31:256-262, 1987), 168 patients with CD were studied, of whom 28% complained of mouth ulcerations from time to time.

Just what kind of cytotoxin or neurotoxin is produced in the intestinal lesions that can travel via the bloodstream and produce ulcers in the mouth we do not know. We must conclude from this study that any person with recurrent apthous stomatitis ulcers should certainly receive the benefit of studies to check on CD and perhaps a trial of a GF diet for several months.

Further Comments

What can we learn from all of the above clinical studies?

Surely, as we have already stated in this book, CD is associated with a far greater number of diseases than medical science ever dreamed could be true. Surely we need to continue to "Think Celiac" whenever we encounter some strange symptoms that are not readily explained.

Further, many more patients need to receive the diet test (the "eating test") for gluten intolerance whenever we come face to face with baffling and perplexing medical problems. The "eating test" is simple, inexpensive, and can be done at home by the patient and his family. But the test requires diligence with elimination of all "cheating" on the diet during the tests.

We also need to remember that though the intestinal biopsy test is quite definitive if it is positive, yet a negative test does not neccessarily rule out celiac disease. Perhaps the biopsy bite was not taken at the ideal spot where the main intestinal problem was located, or perhaps the disease was not in its most ideal stage to be able to expect a positive test. In the end the "eating test" becomes the final arbiter.

Recent advances in blood tests which measure immunoglobulins give promise of possibly becoming standardized and useful in the diagnosis of CD. So, while we wait for these developments, "stay tuned" to whatever clinical news becomes available from time to time.

APPENDIX B

RESOURCES

Celiac Sprue Association/U.S.A., P.O. Box 31700, Omaha, NE 68131-0700, 402 558-0600. The CSA/USA has chapters across the country and can help you find one near you. They also offer a quarterly newsletter with a membership (new members pay $24, renewals after that first year are $20). Call them for a list of products that celiacs can tolerate, cookbook titles and handbooks that are very helpful.

Gluten Intolerance Group of North America, P.O. Box 23053, Seattle, WA 98102, 206 325-6980. Fact sheets and diet instructions for celiacs are available, as well as cookbooks and videotapes. They publish a quarterly newsletter and there are other chapters throughout the country.

Lactaid, Inc., P.O. Box 111, Pleasantville, NJ 08232 or call 1-800 257-8650. Write to them or call between 9:00 a.m. and 5:30 p.m. Eastern time for more information on lactose intolerance and where to find their products.

Ener-G Foods, Inc., P.O. Box 84487, Seattle, WA 98124-5787, 1-800 331-5222, Catalog of gluten-free products available.

RECOMMENDED READING

Gluten Intolerance by Beatrice Trum Hunter, a Good Health Guide published in 1987 by Keats Publishing, Inc., New Canaan, Conn. $1.95.

On the Celiac Condition by Leon Rottmann, Ph.D. This recently revised handbook for celiacs and their families is available for $4 postpaid from the Celiac Sprue Association/U.S.A. in Omaha, Nebraska.

Candida, A Twentieth Century Disease by Shirley S. Lorenzani, Ph.D. includes an anti-yeast diet, therapy program and recipes, along with an excellent overview of related conditions that may be caused by an overgrowth of the *Candida albicans* organism, including irritable bowel symptoms, psoriasis, chronic fatigue and eczema. Published in 1986 by Keats Publishing, Inc., New Canaan, Conn., $3.95.

Candida Albicans by Ray C. Wunderlich, Jr., M.D., and Dwight K. Kalita, Ph.D., a Good Health Guide published in 1984 by Keats Publishing, Inc., New Canaan, Conn., $2.25.

The Candida Albicans Yeast-Free Cookbook by Pat Connolly and Associates of The Price-Pottenger Nutrition Foundation. Published in 1985, this book is a gold mine for candidiasis sufferers, and includes tips on shopping, meal-planning and dining out, lists of foods to avoid and dozens of recipes. Many of the recipes are gluten-free and are suitable for celiacs as well. Keats Publishing, Inc., of New Canaan Conn. publishes this book and it is available for $9.95.